BOJAGI

The Art of Korean Textiles

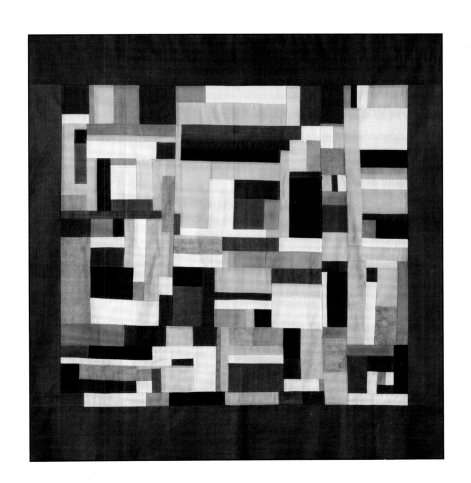

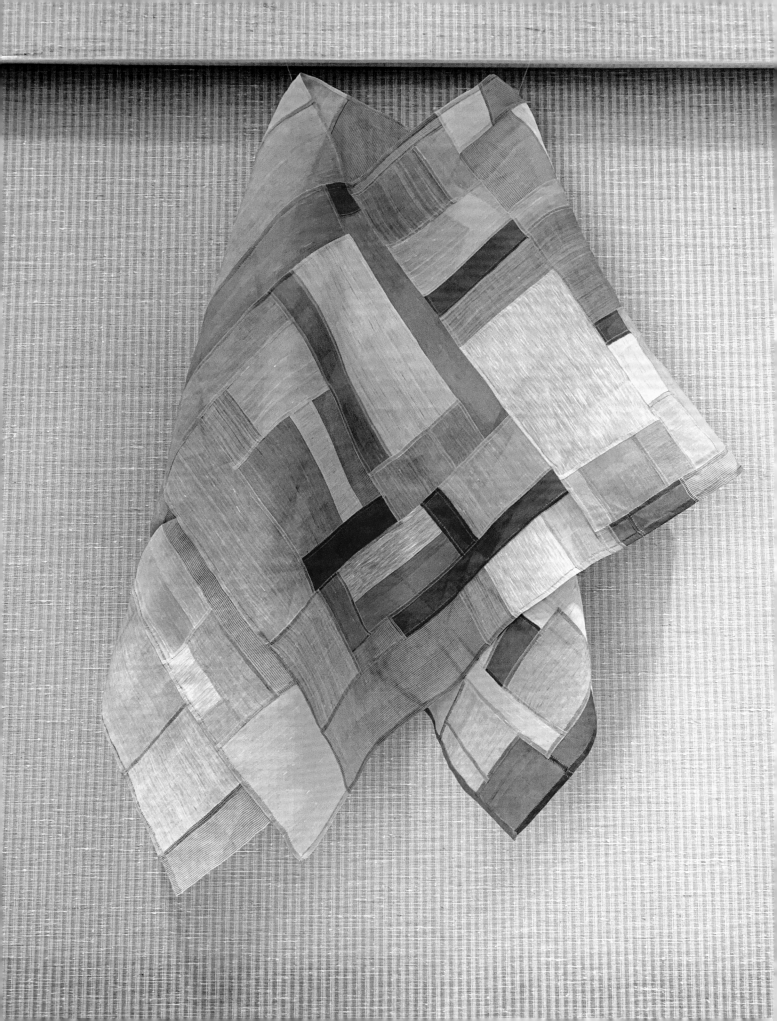

BOJAGI

The Art of Korean Textiles

Youngmin Lee

HERBERT PRESS

LONDON · OXFORD · NEW YORK · NEW DELHI · SYDNEY

HERBERT PRESS
Bloomsbury Publishing Plc
50 Bedford Square, London, WC1B 3DP, UK
29 Earlsfort Terrace, Dublin 2, Ireland

BLOOMSBURY, HERBERT PRESS and the Herbert Press logo are trademarks of
Bloomsbury Publishing Plc

First published in Great Britain in 2024

A catalogue record for this book is available from the British Library
ISBN: 978-1-7899-4183-8; ePub 978-1-7899-4182-1

3 5 7 9 10 8 6 4 2

Design layouts by Lorraine Inglis Design
Printed and bound in Turkey by Elma Basim

To find out more about our authors and books visit www.bloomsbury.com and sign up for our newsletters

Contents

1 Introduction

Textiles hold history, and they have the power to initiate conversation about culture, tradition, time, and memory. I appreciate the beauty that comes from the long, slow process of hand stitching, which is a meditative act for me. I constantly practice stitches on the surface of fabrics and think about the invisible labor done by women throughout time. I use a variety of materials to make items that both reflect modern aesthetics and embrace traditional techniques. This represents my identity as one living in two cultures; bojagi is my interpretation of my cultural heritage and tradition. I create through a spontaneous and improvisational process, using various materials, from new bolts of fabric to reclaimed textiles. I start this organic process by putting small fragments together, and the bojagi and I both grow as I work many imperfect stitches together with my wishes for *haengbok* (영민 – happiness).

I have been wanting to write a book about bojagi for a long time. As I shared bojagi with the people around me, I felt that I needed to organize my thoughts and methodology so I could share my knowledge of and love for the subject properly. When I first started making bojagi, I picked up pieces of fabric to fulfill my desire to make. I soon discovered the unexpected positive side effects of hand-sewing bojagi – I enjoyed sewing and completing a project, but I also found the process had a calming and meditative effect. I often tell people who take my classes, 'Try to find a rhythm in your own stitches.' Instead of trying to make perfect, even stitches, let your fingers and your needle work together. I believe this will help to infuse your good intentions into the bojagi you are making, so the finished object can carry this positive energy on. This is a book about bojagi and my personal journey to find happiness.

Wishing you *haengbok*,

행복을 빌며,

영민

Youngmin Lee

(*Opposite*) Geometric design *jogakbo* made with *sukgosa* (Korean silk gauze) 2014. 22 x 58¼"

When I was a child, I had a box of fabric scraps that I collected from my mom's sewing projects and my aunt's stash of leftovers – my aunt owned a small *hanbok* (Korean traditional clothing) store in Seoul. With my scraps of fabric, my tiny bedroom became a small imaginary fabric store. I admired the various colors and textures of the scraps. My affection for textiles led me to study Clothing and Textiles in college, and Fashion Design at graduate school. After I graduated, I worked in the fashion industry for a few years. When my husband got a job offer overseas, he asked me if I could put my career on pause for about five years, for the chance to live in California. I had fond memories of living in California for about a year in the past, so I agreed to pack up and move from Seoul to the San Francisco Bay Area with my husband and our six-month-old daughter. Back then, when we did *bottari ssada* (packing things in bojagi and moving to another place), my husband and I had no idea that we would stay in the Bay Area for over 26 years.

When I had adjusted to a new place and my daughter began school, I grabbed some fabric from my new stash box (I lost my original fabric box during one of several moves we made after our marriage) and started to make things. I made clothes for my daughter, cloth napkins and dish towels, aprons, and bojagi out of fabric that I brought from Korea. I also tried knitting, crocheting, and hand quilting. These making activities bolstered my confidence and helped me discover what I wanted to do. The act of making made me feel comfortable; Korean silks and ramie especially helped to soothe my homesickness. I had taken some classes about Korean costume history and *hanbok* construction in college, which gave me a good foundation to start making my own bojagi with many different designs and styles. Gradually people around me started to notice my bojagi and asked me questions such as: 'What is that?', 'What is bojagi?', 'How do you use it?', and 'How do you make it?' I decided to explore more and share this unique practice with people eager to learn about Korean textile traditions and making processes.

Bojagi have allowed me the opportunity to share my native culture and arts with not only the next generation of Korean Americans, but also people with many different cultural backgrounds. In 2004, I was invited to the San Francisco Asian Art Museum to participate in the 'Asia Alive' program. This was my first time meeting and engaging with the public about my work. I was at the museum four days a week for four weeks, sharing my bojagi, and Korean textile traditions and culture.

Objects packed in bojagi can be called *bottari*, which is often used to refer to packing up and moving somewhere.

The Asian Art Museum's annual 'Korea Day' celebration presented another opportunity to introduce bojagi to local museum visitors. In 2011, I was invited by a public school that has a Korean immersion program to come and teach bojagi classes to students from the third to the eighth grades. I taught them every year until 2022. In 2014, Los Angeles County Museum of Art (LACMA) invited me to give a talk about bojagi and host some workshops.

The museum also has a vision for engagement with visitors. So, we started the 'Community Bojagi Project' to work with people visiting the museum. Over four months, more than 1,700 people participated and helped us to finish the project.

Jogakbo made with my family's old *hanbok*, such as my mom's *chima* (skirt) and my brother's *durumagi* (outer jacket). By using my family members' old clothes, I was wishing for their happiness and well-being.

The Community Bojagi hanging in the Boone Children's Gallery

Our community bojagi was installed at the Boone Children's Gallery at LACMA. LACMA submitted our project to Guinness World Records, and it is now officially the world's largest bojagi!

I participate in many cultural festivals and events, and people often express their interest and opinions about cultural diversity and similarities between cultures. Teaching bojagi and Korean culture to schoolchildren in local public schools, and leading community bojagi projects at the Los Angeles County Museum and the Asian Art Museum in San Francisco are examples of how I've built a creative community through my cultural experience. I have been participating in the Oakland Museum's Lunar New Year celebration for

two decades, the Asian Art Museum's Korea Day activities for seven years, and Irvine's Korean Festival for four years. I believe that preserving artistic and cultural traditions is a great way to understand and connect communities, and I want to build bridges between cultures. In addition to teaching in person, I created the DVD *Bojagi Wrapping Cloths: The Art of Korean Stitching* in 2013 so that I could reach people from afar.

In both 2019 and 2022, I was fortunate to be a recipient of an apprenticeship supported by the Alliance for California Traditional Arts. I was honored to teach bojagi to my apprentices. By sharing traditional art and craft, I try to connect ancient traditions with contemporary audiences.

Bojagi or pojagi?

I respect and use the Revised Romanization of Korean, the official Korean language romanization system in South Korea. The National Academy of the Korean Language started developing it in 1995, and it was released to the public on 7 July 2000, by South Korea's Ministry of Culture and Tourism in Proclamation No. 2000–8. According to this, 보자기 can be written and pronounced as 'bojagi', and 조각보 as 'jogakbo'.

Colorful *jogakbo* made in the 20th century, with Korean silk

2
What are bojagi?

Bojagi are traditional Korean wrapping cloths. They were used to wrap, cover, carry, or store objects in daily life, on special occasions, and in religious rituals. Koreans believe that bojagi can not only wrap an object but can also enclose *bok* (福, 복, good fortune or happiness). *Seollal* (Lunar New Year's Day) and *Chuseok* are two big Korean holidays, and people visit family and exchange gifts and presents (often nicely wrapped in bojagi).

The act of making bojagi also carries wishes for the well-being and happiness of its recipients. The labor of love and the good wishes felt while making the bojagi imbue the item with the affectionate energy of the maker.

Historical records show that bojagi have been used since very early times. One example comes from the *Samguk Yusa* (Memorabilia of the Three Kingdoms of Korea), which contains legends, folktales and historical accounts related to the Three Kingdoms of Korea (BC57–AD668). These were collected and written by the Buddhist monk Iryeon (1206–1289). The *Legend of Garak* mentions a golden box containing six golden eggs that came down from the heavens, wrapped in *hong pok* (red bojagi). According to legend, the King Suro of Geumgwan Gaya was born from one of these golden eggs.

Fabrics deteriorate over time and with use. Therefore, most old bojagi that have survived are from the Joseon Dynasty (1392–1910), but one

exceptionally old extant bojagi was used to cover the ritual table of the *Daegakguksa* (National Preceptor Grand Enlightenment) Uicheon (1055–1101), a Buddhist priest. The earliest existing bojagi from the Joseon Dynasty are the seven wrapping cloths made by Lady Yi in 1415, to wrap and cover Buddhist sutras in commemoration of her late husband, Yu Kun. These are embroidered wrapping cloths, decorated with Tang scrolls, grasses, trees, clouds and cranes.

Bojagi held an important place in Korean daily life during the Joseon Dynasty, and this continues today. Growing up in Korea, I hardly paid attention to bojagi because of their ubiquitous presence in daily life.

During the rigid and strict Confucian society of the Joseon Dynasty, women were restricted to the house and its inner courtyard. When they did go outside the family compound, they had to cover their faces and heads so as to be invisible. They were not allowed to learn and write as men could. Along with sewing and embroidering, making bojagi must have been one of the few creative outlets they were permitted. Korean women poured their creativity into stitching, to make beautiful pieces that had many different purposes. Bojagi were made for practical reasons, and often had specific uses. The bojagi they created show how women tried to make something both useful and beautiful.

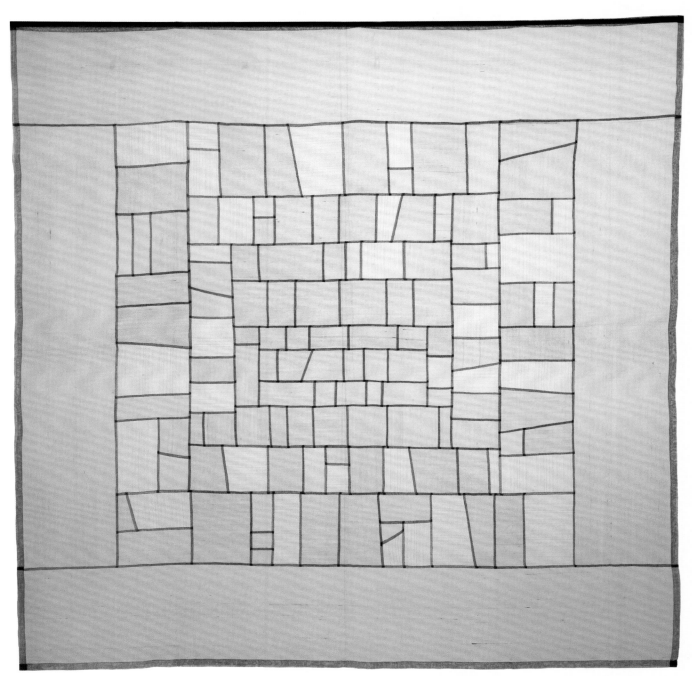

Jogakbo made with *nobang* (silk organza)

Many bojagi of the Joseon Dynasty were made and used by women who were not well educated, but the bojagi they created and used are examples of considered and well-thought-out design and composition.

The process of making bojagi was passed down from generation to generation. Until the 1960s, bojagi were not made to be sold. Instead, they were made with specific recipients in mind, such as soon-to-be-married young maidens who could use or keep the bojagi to remember their family after the marriage. In 2013, when I was teaching a bojagi workshop in Los Angeles, I met journalist Sookee Chung. She showed me a few bojagi that she had brought with her when she moved from South Korea to the USA. These bojagi were her grandmother Chang Sooja's wedding trousseau from the 1930s, passed down to her through her mother. They showed how people recycled remnants of fabrics from items such as handmade projects, bedding, clothes, and other household items. One of the bojagi was made with the selvages from multiple fabrics, featuring some Chinese characters and a horse motif. These

characters show the kind of fabric (*mobondan*), the place the fabric was made (Yeongheung), and the company name. Later, Sookee Chung donated these bojagi to the Asian Art Museum in San Francisco. I was happy to see them again there, and to be able to study them further.

Defining bojagi

Bojagi is an umbrella term for wrapping cloths. Most have a square or rectangular shape. One bojagi can have many names, based on the user or maker's class, its intended use, and the material, techniques and designs used.

One way to define bojagi is to categorize them by the social class of the makers and users. The suffix '*bo*' indicates bojagi.

Social class
Gungbo

During the Joseon Dynasty, a government-run workshop called *Sanguiwon* produced a wide range of different bojagi for royal palace use. *Gungbo* were made with differing materials in varying colors for many uses and occasions. They were used not only to wrap objects but also to indicate formality levels, and to convey respect from the giver to the recipients. Most extant *gungbo* are from the late Joseon Dynasty, and many were made of silk fabrics with elaborate designs or embellishments.

Minbo

Minbo were bojagi made and used by ordinary people, including the gentry (*yangban*) and commoners. Many bojagi were made to serve practical purposes in daily life, and for ceremonial use (e.g. weddings).

Another way to define bojagi is by usage and intent: utilitarian, decorative, ritual, ceremonial, etc. The materials, size, construction, and design were decided by the bojagi's intended purpose.

Bojagi made with the selvages from multiple fabrics

Materials and construction

Materials and methods of construction can also be used to distinguish and categorize bojagi.

Materials
• Silk
• Ramie
• Hemp
• Cotton

Construction
• Technique: *ssamsol, gopsol (kkekki), yeouijumun*
• Finished shape and/or layers: *hotbo* (single-layered bojagi), *gyeopbo* (lined bojagi), *nubibo* (quilted bojagi)

• Embellishments: *jasu* (embroidery), *geumbak* (gold leaf), *chaesaek* (painted), *panyeum* (block printed)
• Patchwork versus whole cloth: *jogakbo*
• Straps/ties: none, 1, 2, or 4
• Colors of visible fabrics or thread: *chunghongbo* (blue and red bojagi)
• Design: geometric versus free-form/improvisational design

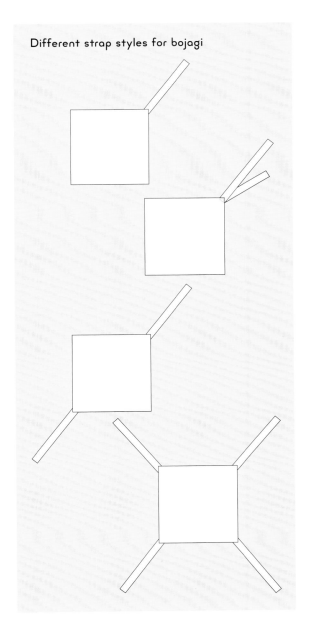

Different strap styles for bojagi

Size

Bojagi are traditionally measured in *pok*, a Korean unit of measurement equivalent to approximately 13¾" [35 cm] in length. Bojagi range in size from 1 to 8, 9, or 10 pok – a larger number means a bigger bojagi.

• A 1-pok bojagi is used for smaller items, e.g. *norigae* bojagi, *yemulbo, gireogibo*
• A 1.5-pok bojagi is used as a covering (*sangbo*)
• A 2-pok bojagi is used to wrap ornaments or smaller boxes
• A 3- or 4-pok bojagi is used for wrapping, carrying and storing larger items, e.g. *ibulbo* (bojagi for bedding), *otbo* (bojagi for clothes), *ppalaebo* (bojagi for laundry)

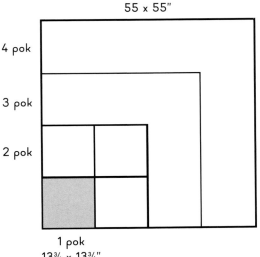

55 x 55"

4 pok

3 pok

2 pok

1 pok
13¾ x 13¾"

Here are some different types of bojagi categorized by their construction, use, materials, and embellishments.

Jogakbo (patchwork bojagi)

Jogakbo, patchwork bojagi, embodies the philosophy of recycling, as the wrapping cloths are made from remnants of leftover fabric. *Jogak* means 'a small piece' in Korean. There are many types of *jogakbo*, defined by the materials used, size, construction, and design. Thoughtfully considered arrangements of different shapes and contrasting colors in the bojagi show Korean women's creative sensibility; they also remind the viewer of abstract compositions, similar to those we often see in contemporary designs.

There are many design options to make *jogakbo*. Here you can see some geometrical patterns, free-form, and improvisational designs.

Some are named by the shape of the *jogak*, or the shape of the design:

- *semo* (triangle)
- *nemo* (square)
- *badukmunbo* (checkerboard pattern)
- *baramgaebimunbo* (pinwheel pattern, log cabin design)
- *dongsimwonbo* (concentric circle)
- *mujigaebo* (rainbow design, made by folding *dongsimwonbo* in half)
- *yeouijumnunbo* (wish-fulfilling jewel pattern, cathedral window pattern)

Some different *jogakbo* designs named by the shape of the *jogak*

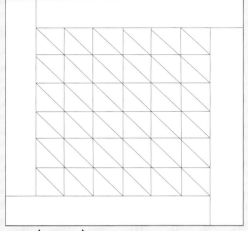

semo (triangle)

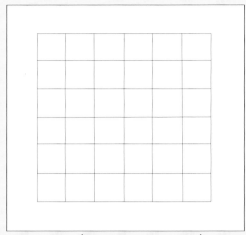

badukmunbo (checkerboard pattern)

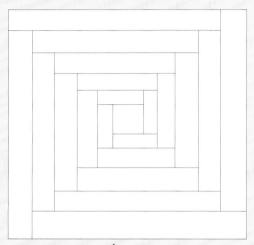

baramgaebimunbo (pinwheel pattern, log cabin design)

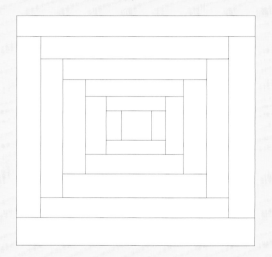

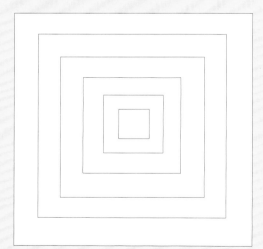

mujigaebo (rainbow design, made by folding *dongsimwonbo* in half)

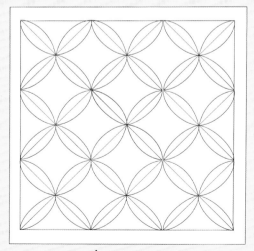

yeouijumnunbo (wish-fulfilling jewel pattern, cathedral window pattern)

Trapezoid shapes are often featured in free-form bojagi. Some are quite large, and I assume these are left over from *hanbok* making. When I see both women's and men's *hanbok* patterns, it seems obvious to me that the trapezoid pieces are remnants from when pattern pieces for jackets and pants were cut. Sometimes I get leftover fabrics from a friend who owns a *hanbok* business and I see the trapezoid pieces in those, too.

I made one *jogakbo* out of remnants from my lotus leaf mat project (see p.72), and while I was making this piece, I enjoyed working with the curvilinear design that was forming from the randomly cut pieces of fabric.

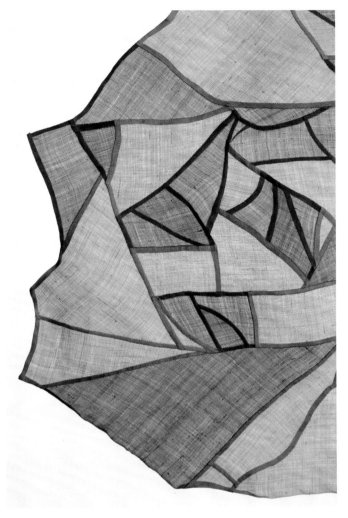

Subo (jasubo, embroidered bojagi)

Subo (embroidered bojagi) were commonly made and used for happy occasions like weddings. *Su* or *jasu* means 'embroidery' in Korean. Some *subo* have straps or ties, others don't. The embroidered motifs vary from natural elements, such as plants and animals, to geometric patterns and lucky symbols and characters. Flowers represent wealth and prosperity; fruits represent abundance in material things and fertility; and birds and butterflies represent happiness and joy. Common characters include longevity, good fortune, happiness, prosperity, fertility, and warding off evil spirits. In many surviving *subo*, the motifs were embroidered on cotton or silk fabric and lined with silk.

A *subo* in my collection

Gireogibo (bojagi for wooden geese)

Gireogibo is the bojagi used during traditional Korean wedding ceremonies. It is used to wrap the wooden geese that the bridegroom presents and places on the table, signifying his vow to the bride's family. *Gireogi*, the wild goose, represents fidelity

and loyalty in Korean culture. Traditionally, red and blue fabrics are used to make the lined (double-layered) *gireogibo*. It is then decorated with embroidery and multi-colored strands of thread symbolizing wishes for abundance in married life, and a knotted decoration called a *gireogi maedeup* (wild goose knot).

My daughter got married last year, and I was so happy to see her and her husband tie the knot after years together. When I made her *gireogibo*, I followed the traditional construction and motifs but chose colors to match the couple's *hanbok*. This *gireogibo* was made with my wishes for my daughter and son-in-law's happy life together.

Sajubo and honseojibo

Saju, the 'four pillars' of birth – year, month, day and hour – are thought to be components that can predict a person's destiny or fate. Therefore, sharing one's *saju* is considered a very important step when Korean people plan a family member's marriage.

Honseo is a letter of marriage proposal from the bridegroom's family to the bride's family. *Saju* and *honseo* were wrapped in special types of bojagi called *sajubo* and *honseojibo*, respectively, and sent by the bridegroom's family to the bride's family.

These are my husband's *saju*, *honseo*, and *sajubo* from our wedding

This is my own *yeongil* and *yeongilbo* – I remember that my father practiced calligraphy for days to write my *yeongil* and this letter to my father-in-law

Yeongilbo

The bride's family chooses an auspicious date (*yeongil*) for the wedding ceremony and then lets the bridegroom's family know. The written *yeongil* is wrapped in a special bojagi called *yeongilbo*, then sent to the bridegroom's family.

Yemulbo

Yemul, a precious object or gift for special occasions, is wrapped in a bojagi called *yemulbo* and sent from the bridegroom's family to the bride's family. Sometimes auspicious symbols and patterns are embroidered on the fabrics, and other times the fabrics are solid colors. The *yemulbo* that I received from my mother-in-law on my wedding day, similar to the one pictured, is one of my most precious bojagi, and I always keep it in a special place.

Yedanbo

The gifts from the bride's family are enclosed in red and blue silk bojagi called *yedanbo*.

Hotbo

A single-layered bojagi. It can be whole cloth bojagi or *jogakbo* made using *ssamsol* or *gopsol (kkekki)*.

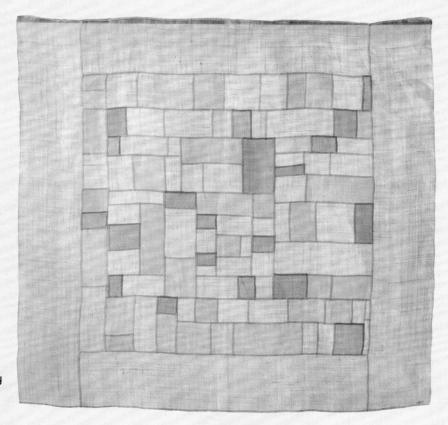

Hotbo made with ramie remnants and ssamsol technique

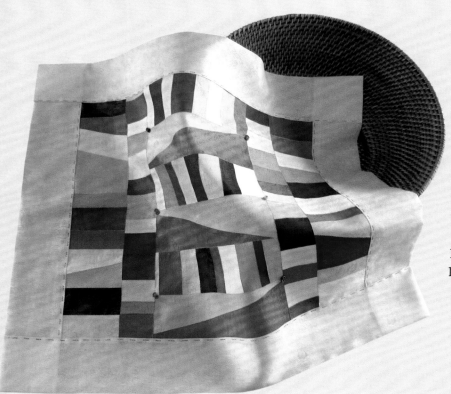

Gyeopbo

Lined bojagi can be made in several ways; for example, using two layers of whole cloth bojagi of different colors, a patchwork top layer and a whole cloth lining, or even an embroidered top layer and a whole cloth lining.

Nubibo

Quilted bojagi are used either to insulate objects or to keep food items warm. *Nubibo* have two or three layers, sometimes including a layer of batting. This is my *nubi sangbo*, given to me by my mother. It is machine quilted and made in Tongyeong, a region well known for its quilting tradition.

Sangbo, sikjibo, matbo

Bojagi to cover the dining table, keep the food warm, or to keep insects away. Most are double-layered *jogakbo* with a lining. There is often a knob or handle in the middle for easy lifting. Sometimes the bojagi, such as *sikjibo* or *matbo*, are lined with oiled paper.

Norigaebo

Norigae is an ornament that women wear with *hanbok*. Many *norigaebo* are silk bojagi with cotton batting, approximately 1 pok in size. They are used to wrap and protect precious and fragile items. One or two sashes/straps are attached on the corner(s) to wrap, tie and secure.

in Western quilting. Yes, they are the same technique! The fabric folding process is similar to that used by schoolchildren to make paper fortune tellers. A base layer is built by folding and connecting multiple identical units. Each quilt block is made using a folded patchwork technique. Often the finished blocks are decorated with *bakjwi maedeup* (bat-shaped knot).

The first documented evidence of the use of cathedral window design in a quilt appeared at the 1933 Chicago World's Fair in the USA, and it quickly became popular in North America. In her book, *Cathedral Window Quilts*, Lynne Edwards made the inference that this technique may have been brought to the USA by missionaries from the East in the early twentieth century – a wonderful example of cross-cultural influence.

Yeouijumunbo

Yeouiju means 'wish-fulfilling jewel', so *yeouijumunbo* can be translated as a jewel-patterned bojagi. Sometimes it is called *gojeonmun*, which means 'old coin pattern'. Old Korean coins were circular with a hole in the middle. This pattern reflects the maker's simple wish for prosperity. *Yeouijumunbo* is one of the *jogakbo* designs found often in bojagi from the Joseon Dynasty period, and it remains popular today.

People often ask me if *yeouijumun* is the same technique as the cathedral window pattern found

Geumbakbo

Geumbak, gold leaf imprinting, is a Korean embellishing tradition used on clothing and textiles. Motifs symbolizing well wishes were imprinted with gold leaf into the surface of the fabric. In the past, *geumbakbo* was mostly found on *gungbo*. Commoners were only allowed to use *geumbakbo* on special occasions. Above is an image of *geumbak* in my *dangui*. A *dangui* is a ceremonial robe that women wear over a *jeogori* (short jacket/top). It has side slits, and its hem lines are curved with pointed edges.

3
Tools

Seven friends

When I introduce my sewing tools, I often refer to them as seven personified sewing friends from an old Korean story: needle, thread, scissors, ruler, corner iron, flat iron, and thimble. I use these simple, yet essential tool friends in my sewing, and store them in the *banjitgori* (반짇고리 – a basket or container used to store sewing tools) that my mother gave me when I got married.

New and modern 'friends' such as a rotary cutter, cutting mat, fabric marker, and needle threader are tools that help my creating process.

There is an old Korean story about Lady Ju's seven friends – a ruler, a pair of scissors, a needle, thread, a thimble, a small iron with a long handle (*indu*, a narrow, triangular-shaped tip that flattens seams or corners), and a flat iron (*darimi*, a flat-bottomed bowl-shaped iron that holds hot charcoal). These seven friends were arguing about who helps the lady the most and was therefore her best friend. They all insisted, 'I am the best friend of my lady, because...'

> 'Without me, how can she measure and know if it's too long or too short?' said the ruler.
> 'But I can cut precisely,' said the scissors.
> 'If I am not fast, how can she make neat stitches?' said the needle.
> 'But she can't stitch without me!' said the thread.
> 'Without my support, our lady's finger gets tired quickly,' said the thimble.

> 'I make small seams look as nice as if they were glued together,' said the small iron.
> 'But you only can help a little,' said the flat iron to the small iron. 'I can remove all the wrinkles from the cloth.'

After they were scolded by the lady, the seven friends realized that they needed to help each other and collaborate to best help the lady's sewing work.

Thread

I use various kinds of threads, made from both natural and synthetic fibers, to make bojagi. 40wt or 50wt cotton threads are versatile. For basting, you can use heavier-weight cotton thread. Linen thread, which is difficult to find in sewing supply stores, requires a conditioner such as thread wax or beeswax. Hemp thread is also hard to find and, like linen, needs to be treated with wax, so I don't use it much. I like to use silk thread for bojagi making. I use 50wt silk thread for hand piecing and finishing bojagi. Silk threads in heavier weights (30wt, 16wt and 9wt) are used for decorative stitches such as *settam sangchim* (see p.46). Silk thread is strong but tends to bleed color when wet. One must be careful if using silk thread for practical or utilitarian bojagi. Traditionally, threads were matched to fabrics, for example, cellulose fibers for cotton, linen, ramie, or hemp fabrics, and silk threads for silk fabrics, but since I make both practical and art bojagi, I don't strictly follow this rule. When I make bojagi as artwork, I often use various types of thread and fabrics.

Needles

A needle is a must-have tool, and I keep a wide variety of types and sizes close at hand. A sharp, small-eyed needle is my favorite, because it doesn't leave puncture marks on fabric. I use one of these for fine fabrics like silk. For ramie, hemp, or linen I use a longer needle. To make decorative stitches with thicker thread, use an embroidery/crewel needle. Try different needles and use the one that is comfortable for you.

Scissors

8" [20 cm] fabric scissors are used to cut or trim fabric. The smaller embroidery scissors and thread snippers are useful to trim off threads or cut small bits of fabric.

Ruler

There are various sizes of rulers with grids, which are helpful to measure sizes and check straight lines. A tape measure is useful as well.

Thimbles (*Golmu*)

Iron

I often emphasize the importance of ironing between piecing steps. Keeping fabrics neat and tidy makes such a difference, especially when you are dealing with small pieces of fabric to create *jogakbo*. For some seam techniques such as *ssamsol* or *gopsol* (*kkekki*), ironing between steps is critical to produce fine seam lines.

A corner iron (*indu*) is helpful when folding small pieces of fabric and shaping curved lines.

Thimble (golmu)

A sturdy thimble protects your finger when you push the needle through layers of fabrics. I make my own thimbles using scraps of fabrics and reinforce them with *baejeopji* (multiple layers of muslin and *hanji* – Korean mulberry paper).

In the old days, a bride would make 100 thimbles before her marriage and bring them all with her to her husband's house to use while sewing, or give away as gifts to female family members in the household.

New friends – nice-to-have tools

- Bone folder (creaser) is a useful tool to make creases to mark seam allowances.
- Pins are essential to hold layers of fabrics. Extra-fine pins are good because they don't damage fine, lightweight fabrics. Longer pins (about 2" [5 cm] or longer) are useful to roll fabrics when making *bakjwi maedeup* (bat-shaped knot).
- Fabric marker: chalk pencil, heat erasable pens, water soluble pens, etc.
- Rotary cutter and cutting mat make it fast and easy to cut very precise measurements, sizes, or straight lines.

From left to right: pins on a pincushion, bone folders, fabric markers, rotary cutters, seam roller. At the bottom: threader for fine-eyed needles. All placed on a cutting mat.

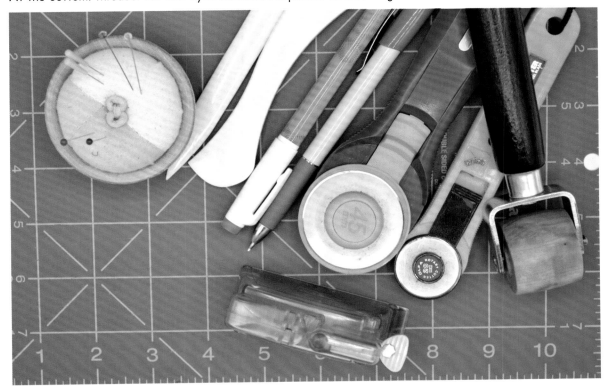

4
Colors and Patterns

Color

When you see bojagi or other traditional Korean textiles, the use of strong, bold colors makes a striking first impression. The five Korean traditional colors are known as '*obangsaek*', inspired by the Korean concept of *Eumyang-Ohaeng* (literally, *yin-yang* and the five elements). Koreans traditionally believed that the world originated from the two forces, *yin* and *yang*. These forces created the *Ohaeng*, or five elements: wood, fire, earth, metal, and water. *Obang*, the five directional (cardinal) colors – black, blue, red, white, and yellow – represent the five elements and directions. Black symbolizes north and water; blue, east and wood; red, south and fire; white, west and metal; and yellow, center and earth. This traditional color symbolism is intertwined in Korean people's everyday lives. Everything from *banchan* (Korean side dishes) and the five-colored garnish on wedding-day noodles, to *saekdong* (see p.32) used in children's garments, are examples of this.

Repelling or protecting against evil is also very important in Korean culture and traditions. Certain colors and patterns are thought to have this power – for example, red is a *yang* color, and repels badness. For good luck and protection, Koreans make and eat red bean porridge on the winter solstice, and tie a rope with red peppers and charcoal in front of a house with a newborn baby. They even tie a similar rope around pots of freshly made soybean paste. *Ogansaek* (pink, purple, sulphur yellow, light blue, green) are expanded color palettes used with *obangsaek*.

Obangsaek – the five cardinal colors: black, blue, red, white and yellow

Pattern

Living a long, healthy and prosperous life with a loving family would be considered a happy life by most. These things are the best that people can hope and wish for. Peace in the afterlife is also hoped for, as is success in casting out evil spirits and badness. To this end, Korean people often use auspicious symbols and patterns in hopes of making these wishes come true.

Longevity is pursued by using the ten Korean longevity symbols: the sun, mountain, water, rock, cloud, pine tree, elixir plant, tortoise, crane and deer. Sometimes the moon, bamboo and peach are added to these ten symbols. Here are some patterns commonly seen in woven fabrics, embroidery, or *geumbak* (gold print).

Fabric with peach, pomegranate and Buddha's hand pattern

Fabric with *geumbak*

Fabric with a phoenix pattern

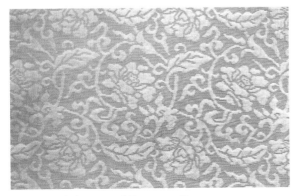
Fabric with lotus and Tang scroll pattern

Sometimes, only one pattern was used; other times, multiple patterns were used together to make a larger, more intricate pattern, such as *doryubulsumun* (peach, pomegranate and Buddha's hand), *unhakmun* (clouds and crane), *morandangcho* (peony and Tang scroll), *Bonghwangmun* (phoenix), and the list goes on.

In *doryubulsumun*, the peach represents longevity, pomegranates symbolize fertility, and the Buddha's hand pattern means good luck in both one's current life and the afterlife.

Korean holidays

Seollal (Lunar New Year)

Seollal (Lunar New Year; first day of the lunar calendar) is one of the most celebrated national holidays in Korea. More than just a holiday to mark the beginning of a new year, *Seollal* is a truly special occasion for Korean people. It is a time for paying respect to ancestors, and an opportunity to catch up with family members. *Seolbim* means new clothes, especially *hanbok*, for *Seollal*. During *Seollal*, Koreans usually wear *Seolbim*, perform ancestral rites, play folk games, prepare foods such as rice cake soup with *mandu* (dumplings offered to the ritual table) to remember and honor ancestors, visit family, eat together, and exchange wishes for good fortune in the New Year. Gifts are usually wrapped and carried in inexpensive pink bojagi.

This is my brother and me in the 1970s in *saekdong hanbok*. When I was young, my aunt who owned a *hanbok* store in Seoul sent us *hanbok* for *Seolbim* or *Chuseokbim* every year.

Chuseok (Harvest Full Moon Festival)

Chuseok, Korean Thanksgiving Day, is another big holiday in Korea. Family members from near and far come together to share food and to give thanks to their ancestors. Many Koreans visit their hometowns to spend time with family. The holiday also presents opportunities to enjoy traditional cultural Korean experiences. New clothes for the *Chuseok* are *Chuseokbim*.

The food most associated with *Chuseok* is *songpyeon* – small dumplings made with rice flour dough, shaped into small balls, and filled with sesame seeds, beans, red beans, chestnuts, or other nutritious ingredients. When steaming the *songpyeon*, the rice cakes are layered with pine needles, which adds a delightful fragrance. It is an old tradition, where the entire family gathers to make *songpyeon* together on the eve of *Chuseok*. An old Korean superstition says that one who makes beautifully shaped *songpyeon* will find a good spouse or give birth to a beautiful baby.

On my daughter's first birthday in 1996, she wore her *dolbok* – a *hanbok* specially for a child's first birthday. She is wearing *saekdong dangui* (long jacket), *chima* (skirt) and *jobawi* (headdress made with black silk and *geumbak*).

Beoseon, Korean socks (top) and Saekdong shoes for toddlers (bottom)

Saekdong (색동) is a multi-colored striped fabric often used for children's *hanbok* (*jeogori, durumagi,* or *dangui*) for their first birthday and holidays. *Saek* means color, and *Dong* means a stripe or a unit of the fabric piece. These colorful stripes are intended to protect children from evil spirits and repel bad luck. They also convey wishes for happiness, good luck, and longevity.

5
Materials

Traditional Korean fabrics

Various kinds of fabrics are traditionally used to make bojagi. Bojagi materials are closely tied to the fabrics used to make clothes, since many were remnants from making clothes. Traditionally, clothes were made for the distinctive four seasons in Korea. Spring and fall *hanbok* were made with thin silks such as silk gauze (*sukgosa*), patterned fine silk gauze (*gapsa*), or plain, opaque silk fabric (*myeongju*), and lined with lighter weight silks such as organza (*nobang*). Summer clothes were made using a single layer of ramie or hemp. Winter clothes were made with heavier-weight silks (*dan*) or cotton, or quilted with cotton batting.

From front to back: *mumyeong* (cotton), *mosi* (ramie), *sambe* (*Andongpo* hemp), *sambe* (hemp)

In modern times, fabrics such as linen and blended fabrics (*gyojik*) are also used. I like to use *chunpo* (ramie/silk or hemp/silk) and *hanjibidan* (mulberry paper yarn/silk). These are wonderful materials for expressing creative ideas. Synthetic materials can also be used but, given the choice, I prefer to use natural fibers.

I also like to use fabrics purchased from local stores. I am fortunate to have wonderful fabric stores in my area, and I enjoy searching for interesting materials for new work; it makes me feel alive and creative! Sometimes, I repurpose materials from old clothes, bed linens and materials given to me by my family or friends. I also experiment with natural dyeing processes in my backyard. Marigold petals, onion skin, avocado pits and eucalyptus leaves are easy to find and to dye materials with. Indigo needs a bit of preparation and practice, but I like to expand my horizons, and there are so many ways to achieve more colors.

Silk (bidan)

Silk is a natural filament fiber from silkworm cocoons, and Korean silk comes from the mulberry silkworm (*Bombyx mori*). Silk fiber contains two substances: fibroin and sericin. Fibroin is a structural protein, and sericin is a gummy substance that surrounds it. Silk that contains

Various kinds of sa (silk gauze) and *mundan* (patterned damask on satin)

Chunpo (ramie and silk blend fabric)

both fibroin and sericin has some structure and stiffness. *Oksa* (slub silk), *nobang* (organza), and raw silk are in this category.

The process of removing sericin is called 'degumming'. Degummed silk fiber is soft and lustrous. Silk chiffon is a delicate degummed silk fabric with a soft drape.

There are many different types of silk fabrics in Korea. Their names can depend on weave structure, pattern, or whether they are degummed. *Ju* refers to plain (tabby) woven fabric, *sa* means gauze (leno) weave, and *dan* is satin weave. Raw silk fiber is called *saengsa*, and boiled, degummed silk fiber is called *suksa*, from *saeng* (fresh) and *suk* (boiled).

Oksa is silk fabric that has an irregular slub texture. It is created using fiber from a double cocoon – two silkworms in one cocoon. The fiber varies in thickness, resulting in the irregular appearance and texture.

These are photos from the 2019 Korea Textile Tour, an annual event that I run, which explores Korean culture and textile traditions. I visited Sangju Heossi Bidan, a silk manufacturing company that has been running for five generations.

I've been collecting different types of fabrics for some time and have made my own reference book of Korean fabrics. Many of the fabric names are based on the material, weave, and patterns. I was fascinated by the subtle differences between each fabric. I hope you will also enjoy learning about these beautiful materials.

Mr. Heo's museum: This image shows how cocoons were raised and stored in the old days.

Mr. Heo demonstrating how to get silk filaments from cocoons.

The silk filaments reeled into silk skein.

Mr. Heo weaves silk on an old loom.

Woven silk fabrics are scoured and dried in this room, so that the pristine texture and surface are protected.

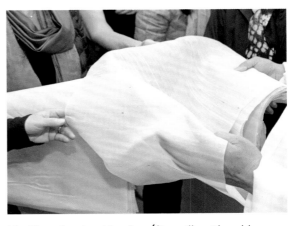

Mr. Heo showing his *oksa* (fine silk with nubby texture) to the 2019 Korea Textile Tour guest.

Ju – plain weave silk fabrics

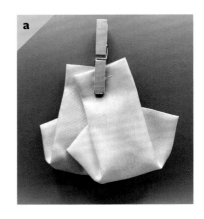

a *Myeongju* is a solid, opaque plain weave silk.

b *Saeng myeongju* is *myeongju* weave with raw silk thread. The texture is rougher and more translucent than *myeongju*.

c *Hongdukkae myeongju* is a plain weave silk processed with starch and fulled, which involves pounding the woven fabric with wooden pins. It has a lustrous moiré effect on the surface. *Hongdukkae* is a wooden rolling pin used for pounding and smoothing the fabric.

d *Nobang* (organza) is a plain weave silk made with raw silk thread. It has a smooth surface and stiff texture and is used for summer clothes and linings of *hanbok*. Layered *nobang* creates a moiré pattern.

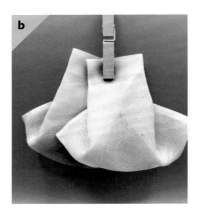
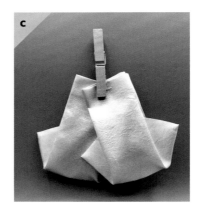

Sa – gauze (leno) weave fabrics

These silks are light, airy, and translucent.

e *Oksa* has an irregular slub texture on the surface.

f *Saenghwasa* is raw silk gauze with a flower pattern (*saeng* meaning 'raw silk', *hwa* meaning 'flower'). It is transparent and lightweight – perfect for summer clothing.

g *Yeondangsa* is a gauze with lotus and Tang scroll patterns.

h *Hwajomun Guksa* is a flower and bird patterned gauze.

i *Hangna* is a weft-ribbed gauze with a stripe-like pattern. A combination of plain weave and warp twisting makes weft-direction ribs.

j *Sukgosa* is degummed gauze with patterns. Auspicious symbols such as gourds, clouds and longevity characters are often used.

k *Hwamun sukgosa* is *sukgosa* with a flower pattern.

l *Jinjusa* is raw silk gauze with a continuous pearl-like pattern (*jinju* meaning 'pearl'). In addition, small motifs of flowers, butterflies and Chinese characters are woven together.

m *Hwasumun jamisa* is a pattern consisting of small *jamihwa* (zinnia flowers) and longevity characters.

n *Eunjosa* is a plain gauze with raw silk thread for the warp, and degummed silk thread for the weft. The contrast between the raw silk thread and the degummed thread makes fine stripes, creating a moiré effect when layered.

o *Sunin* is a gauze weave without any auspicious symbols or patterned background. Plain weave and simple gauze weave make a pattern that looks like fish scales. *Sunin* with auspicious patterns is called *gapsa*.

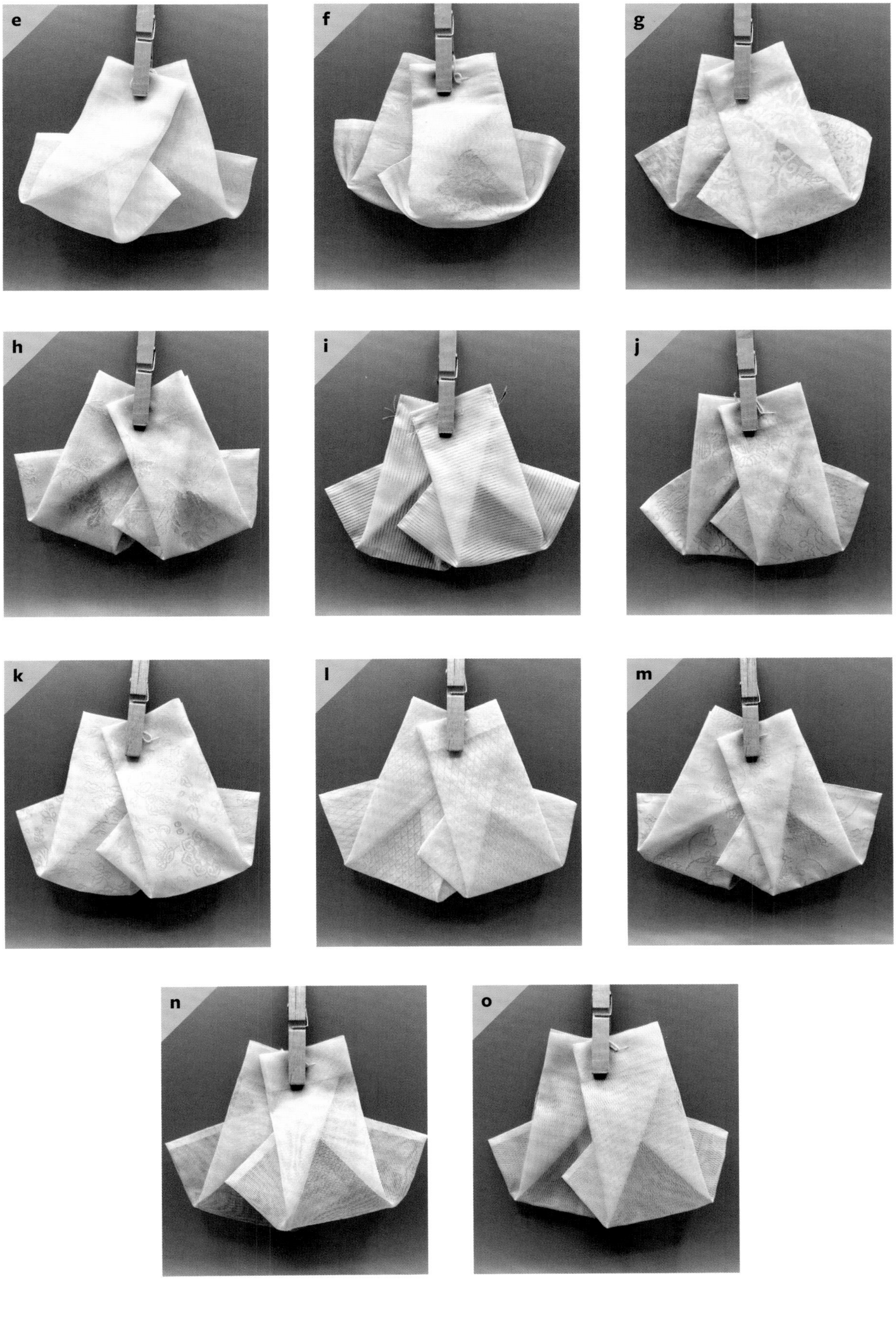
e
f
g
h
i
j
k
l
m
n
o

Gapsa – patterned fine silk gauze

A combination of plain and gauze weaves form a design that looks like a turtle's shell. *Gapsa* often incorporates auspicious patterns such as dragons, clouds, gourds, cranes, phoenixes, butterflies, flowers and Chinese characters.

p *Yong gapsa* big pattern – *gap* means 'turtle' and *yong* means 'dragon'. This *gapsa* fabric has a bigger dragon pattern.

q *Yong gapsa* small pattern – this has the same name as previous fabric but shows a smaller dragon pattern.

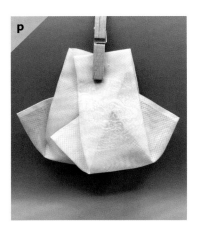 

Dan – a shiny satin weave

Gongdan is a plain surface satin and *mundan* is a damask on satin. They have many names, depending on their pattern, color and weave structure. *Dan* is used for fall and winter clothing in Korea.

r *Gongdan* has a surface that is shiny and smooth.

s *Bonghwangdan* incorporates a phoenix pattern.

t *Unmundan* has a cloud pattern.

u *Yeonhwadan* features a lotus pattern.

v *Podomundan* has a grape pattern.

w *Mobondan* has a peony pattern.

x *Hahwamorandan* has a lotus and peony pattern.

y *Bakjwidan* uses a bat pattern.

z *Jangjidan* has a door frame pattern.

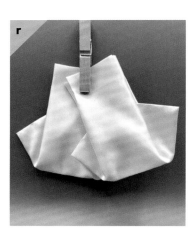 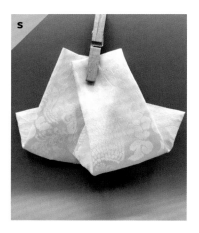 

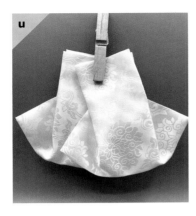

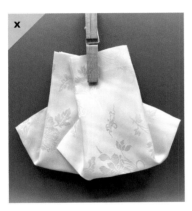

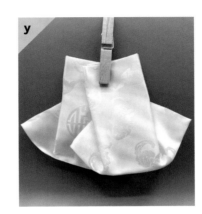

Ramie (mosi)

Ramie (*Boehmeria nivea*) is a tall perennial member of the nettle family. Ramie is cultivated for its long fibers, which are used to make woven textiles. Ramie grows well in the hot and humid climates of the south-western part of South Korea, and other Asian countries. The Hansan region is renowned for its high-quality ramie fabric. Making ramie is very labor intensive. First, ramie stems are cut from

A traditional Korean loom to weave ramie, hemp, and cotton

the plant and the leaves removed. The tops of the stems are snapped, and the outer and inner layers separated, then the stems are bundled together and left to dry in the sun. The drying process can take several days; every morning, the fibers are soaked in fresh water, before drying in the sun again. Then they are soaked in water for a final time, and split into very thin fibers using hands and teeth. To make a long skein of thread, the ramie fibers are combined with the maker's saliva and twisted together by rubbing them on one knee. The resulting ramie thread is called *mosi gut*.

In order to weave one *pil* (a bolt of ramie about 24 yards [22 m] long), 20 skeins of *mosi gut* are needed (ten for warp and ten for weft). The process takes about two months, from the cutting of the ramie plant to weaving it into fabric. The finished ramie fabric measures approximately 12" [30 cm] wide. Finely woven ramie fabric is very durable, with a lustrous sheen and an airy quality. It absorbs moisture and dries fast, so it is suitable for warm-weather clothing.

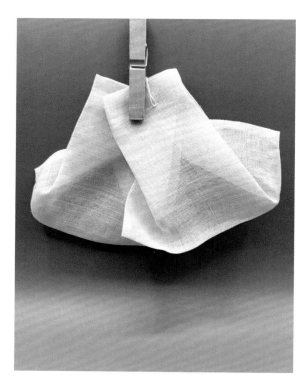

Hemp (sambe)

Hemp (*Cannabis sativa*) is an annual plant that grows to around 6–10 feet [2–3 m] in height. Hemp is very easy to grow and can be grown anywhere in South Korea. Commoners cultivated and wove it into fabric for clothing during the Joseon Dynasty. Woven hemp is a wonderful moisture-wicking fabric, suitable for summer clothing and bedding. While ramie was used to make clothing for the nobility, hemp was ordinary people's everyday material. Hemp has a natural golden color and is very durable. The Andong region is well known for quality hemp fabrics, or *Andongpo*. *Andongpo* is also known to make the best quality burial and mourning clothes.

Like ramie, the processing of hemp fabric is laborious work. Hemp is harvested in the summer by cutting stalks, removing leaves, and tying the stalks into bunches. These bunches are steamed in a specially made pit (*samgut*). The bunches of steamed hemp are untied and left to dry in the sun, then soaked in water and peeled, then sun-dried again. Next, the stalks are scoured by boiling them with lye. *Andongpo* skips this process, so this fiber is called *saengnaengi* (non-boiled fiber). Again, the

maker uses their teeth to split the stalks, making long, thin, hair-like threads, which they then twist together by rubbing them against their knee or thigh. A paste made of soybeans is applied during this process so that fibers are well connected and smooth. The skeins of thread are dried and are then ready to be woven into fabric 1 pok wide. The finished fabric is washed and bleached, turning it from a reddish color to a natural golden yellow. It can be bleached several times to achieve a paler fabric.

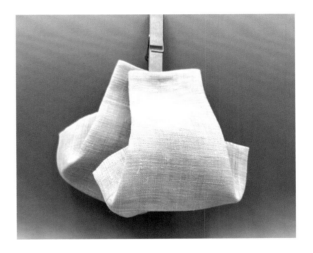

Cotton (myeonpo)

Cotton is a cellulose fiber harvested from the cotton boll. *Mumyeong* is plain handwoven cotton. It has a coarse, uneven texture from the hand weaving process, and usually comes in a narrow width of about 12½–14" [32–36 cm] (**a**).

Linen (ama)

Linen (or flax) is an annual plant that is cultivated as both a fiber crop and for food. Linen is the fabric woven from the flax fibers. It has a stiff texture, wrinkles easily, and is very durable. Linen is easy to find in many places in the world, and I think it is a good substitute for ramie or hemp in bojagi making (**b**).

Fabric blends (gyojik)

Hanji bidan is a blended fabric with silk for the warp and *hanji* (Korean mulberry paper) for the weft (**c**).

Chunpo is a blend fabric with silk for the warp and *mosi* for the weft. Sometimes, *sambe* is used for the weft (**d**).

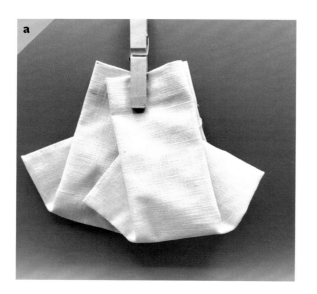

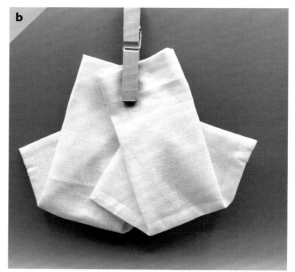

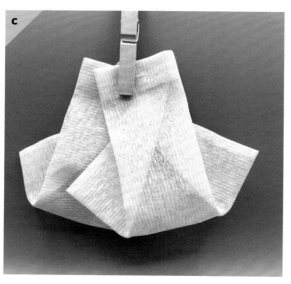

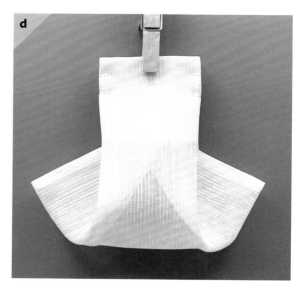

6
Techniques

Stitching techniques

1. Homjil (홈질): Running stitch

Homjil is the simplest and most basic stitch, where the needle goes in and out of the fabric at evenly spaced intervals. With right sides facing, place two layers of fabric together, and stitch on the marked seam line. *Homjil*, along with *gamchimjil*, are techniques used to join pieces of fabric for the top layer of double-layered bojagi.

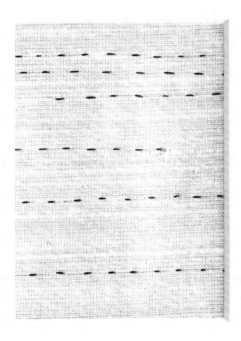

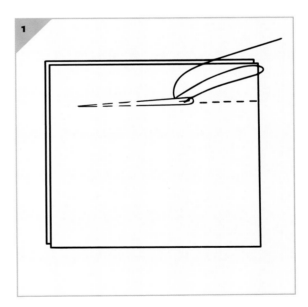

2. Sichimjil (시침질): Basting or tacking stitch

Sichimjil is a long, even running stitch that is used to temporarily secure multiple layers of fabric. There are two types of *sichimjil* – straight and slanted.

3. Gamchimjil (감침질): Whip stitch

Gamchimjil has slanted stitches that show on the fabric's surface. It is known as whip stitch, fell stitch or hem stitch in English.

Placing the folded seam allowances together, you will stitch on the right side of the fabric. Bring the needle through the fabric from the back to the front and repeat as your hand makes a circular motion.

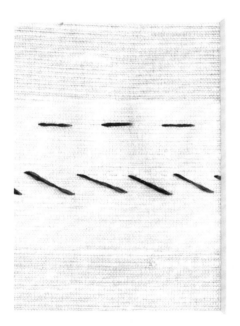

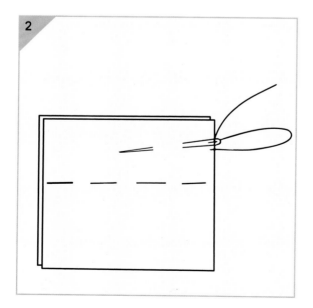

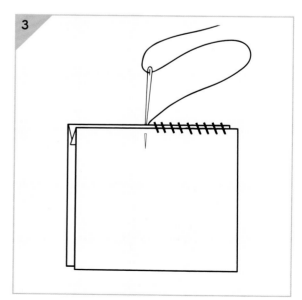

The stitches should be evenly spaced, sized, and tensioned. If the stitch sizes are too large, spaced unevenly, or the tension is too tight, the finished surface won't look flat or smooth.

When using *gamchimjil*, first finger-press the seam allowance toward the wrong side of the fabric, then line up the folded edges of the two pieces together. Create very small, narrow whip stitches along the seam line, so that when the seam is opened and pressed flat, the stitches lie flat next to each other. In bojagi making, using thread of a different color for the *gamchimjil* creates an eye-catching contrast between the fabric pieces and the thread.

4. Bageumjil (박음질): Back stitch

Bageumjil is a durable, sturdy stitch used for seams and visible stitches.

Stitch up through the fabric about ⅛" [3 mm] or 1 stitch length to the left of the edge of the fabric. Bring the needle back to the edge and stitch down, and then bring the needle up 1 stitch length to the left of the first stitch (the needle and thread will make a 'T' shape). Pull the needle through and continue, always inserting the needle at the end of the previous stitch.

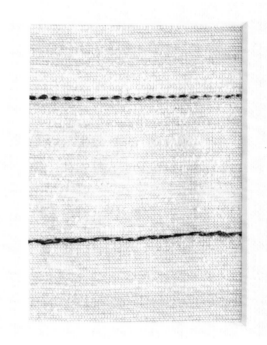

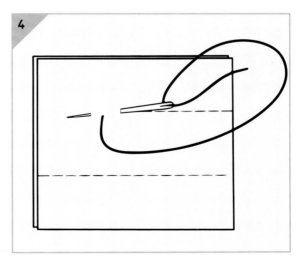

5. Ban bageumjil (반박음질): Half back stitch or spaced back stitch

Stitch up through the fabric about ⅛" [3 mm] or 1 stitch length to the left of the edge of the fabric. Go back about halfway to the edge of the fabric and stitch down, and then bring the needle up 1 stitch length to the left of the first stitch (the needle and thread will make the shape of a letter T). Pull the needle through and continue. Unlike back stitch, instead of inserting the needle at the end of the previous stitch, always leave a small space when you go back. This looks like *homjil* from the front, but is a sturdier stitch.

6. Sangchim (상침): Top stitch

Sangchim is a decorative top stitch using *bageumjil*. Clusters of three consecutive stitches with spaces in between are called *settam sangchim* (*settam* meaning three stitches and *sangchim* meaning top stitch). *Settam sangchim* is used both for securing layers of fabrics and as decoration. Often, contrasting colors of thread are used. You can also use *duttam sanchim* (two decorative top stitches).

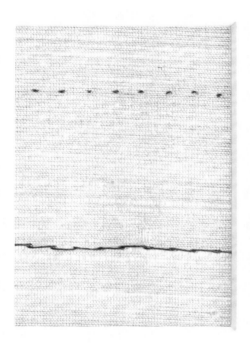

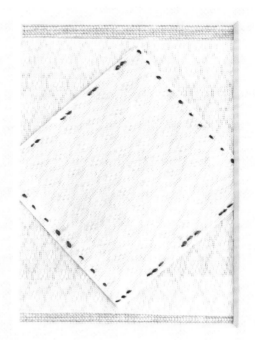

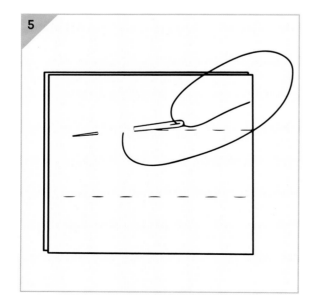

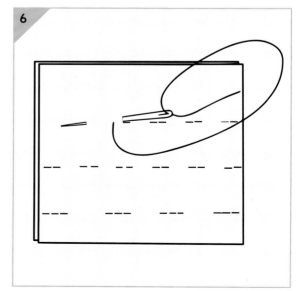

7. Gonggeureugi (공그르기): Blind stitch or slip stitch

Gonggeureugi is used to close openings or for hemming. The stitches are hidden inside the seam allowance and only show tiny marks from the outside. Even tension and stitch length are important to create a smooth surface.

8. Saebaltteugi (새발뜨기): Herringbone stitch

Saebaltteugi is a cross stitch used for hemming. *Saebal* means 'bird's foot', and the name comes from the finished shape of the stitch. Begin with a tiny back stitch from left to right, and make an X shape with your stitches as you continue.

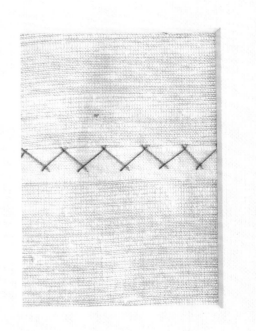

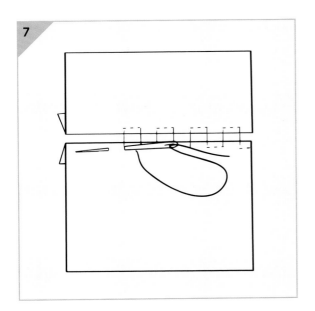

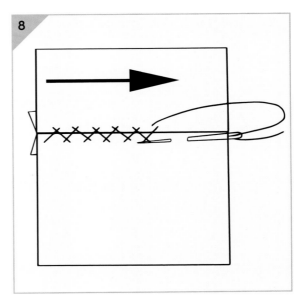

9. Satteugi (사뜨기): Cross stitch

Satteugi connects two finished edges. Elongated X-shape stitches form a thick, raised seam that looks like braided hair. It is a very sturdy yet decorative way of connecting edges. Thicker thread is more effective for this stitch. You can see *satteugi* used on *glomu* (thimble), *jumeoni* (pouch), and *gireogibo* (bojagi for wooden geese).

Start with your needle and thread at the bottom of the left-hand edge, and make three or four straight stitches in parallel lines. Then take the needle and thread upwards to the right-hand edge, take a stitch directly across to the upper left edge, then come back to the bottom right. Stitch across to the left and repeat the steps above.

10. Kkojipgi (꼬집기): Pin tuck stitch, or pinching stitch

Kkojipgi is a very effective technique to show decorative lines. I often use this technique to form gentle curved lines to make a lotus leaf mat (see the project on p.72).

Draw a line or shape and pinch it to raise the line. Then, use *homjil* or *gamchimjil* right below the raised line to make textured outlines.

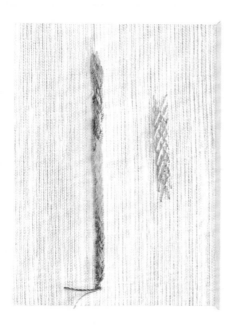

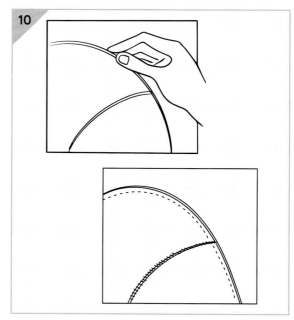

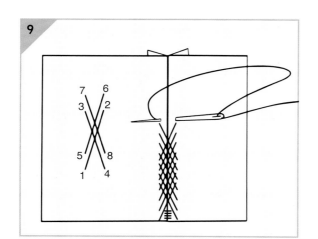

Seam techniques

Of the following techniques, *hotsol* and *gareumsol* are used to make *gyeopbo* (lined bojagi), while *tongsol*, *gopsol* and *ssamsol* are used for *hotbo* (single-layered bojagi).

1. Hotsol (홑솔)

A plain seam with both seam allowances lying in the same direction. *Hot* means 'one'. When bojagi are finished with borders around the pieced block, both seam allowances are pressed toward the border.

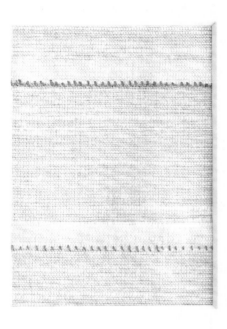

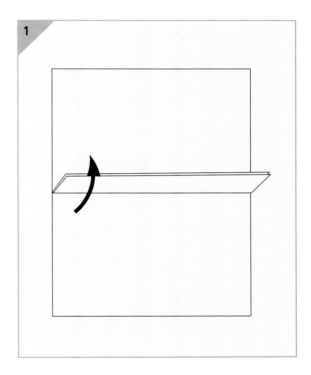

2. Gareumsol (가름솔): Open seam

Seam allowances are pressed open after the fabrics are stitched together. When this seam is made with lightweight fabrics, dispersed seam allowances on each side will give shadow and depth, which I think can be a good design element. For heavier fabrics, this seam will not bulge or cause an uneven surface on the right side of the bojagi.

3. Tongsol (통솔): French seam

This seam encloses the raw edges inside the seam and is useful for lightweight fabrics.

With wrong sides together, sew the seam line on the right side of the fabric. Turn the fabrics so that the right sides are together and press. Sew the seam line, enclosing the raw edges.

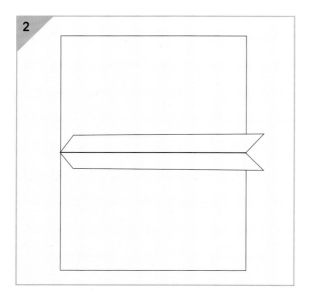

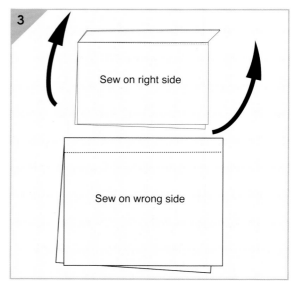

Sew on right side

Sew on wrong side

4. Gopsol (곱솔) or Kkekki (깨끼): Triple stitched seam

Gopsol is a very effective seam for lightweight or sheer fabrics. The finished seam is fine, precise, and sturdy. It can be done both by hand and with a sewing machine.

1. Place two pieces of fabric right sides facing together, sew, and fold the stitched line.

2. Press the folded line and sew the four layers together just over $\frac{1}{16}$" [2 mm] below the previous line. Trim off the rest of the seam allowance as close as possible to the second stitched line.

3. Fold the second stitched line downward and press with an iron or a seam roller.

4. Stitch the third line in between the first and the second stitch line.

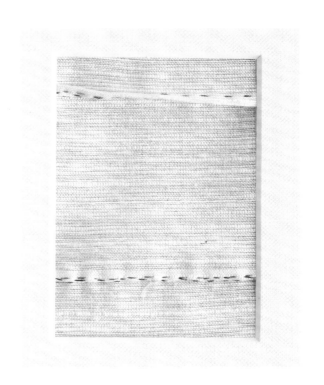

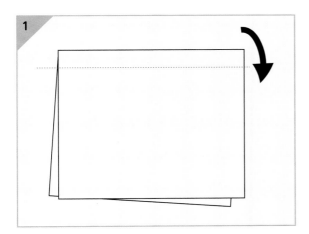

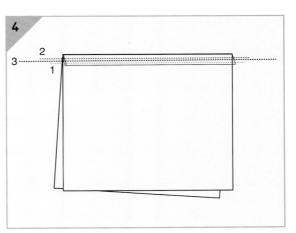

Ssamsol (쌈솔): Flat felled seam

Ssamsol is a durable seam that is often used to make *hotbo* (unlined, single-layered bojagi). The finished seams look identical on both sides. This is an introduction to the basic *ssamsol* technique, using two *gamchimjil*. More detailed instructions for the *ssamsol* technique are covered in the 'Ssamsol 101' on p.62.

1. Prepare the fabric pieces with two different seam allowances. One seam allowance is twice the width of the other, so that it will cover the narrower seam allowance.

2. Fold the seam allowances over towards the wrong side (WS) of the fabric.

3. Place the folded seam allowances together and sew with *gamchimjil* from the right side (RS), making evenly slanted stitches.

4. Press to open the seam, then move the wider seam allowance down toward the narrower seam allowance to cover the edge and score a line in the middle of the wider seam.

5. Fold down the wider seam allowance to encase the narrower seam. Score another line right at the edge of the fold of the wider seam allowance and fold back the fabric so you can see two folded edges. Sew another line with *gamchimjil* at the edge of these two folds. Unfold and press to make the seam flat.

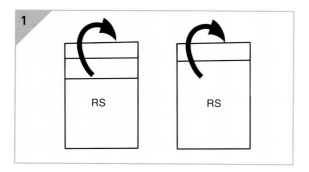

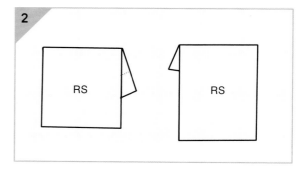

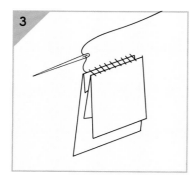

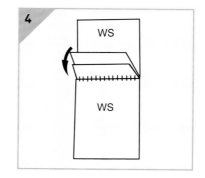

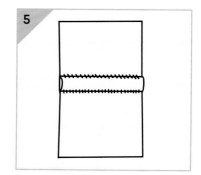

Double-fold hem

1. Fold the hem allowance to the wrong side of the fabric twice.

2. Score at the fold line, and fold toward the right side.

3. Secure the hem using *gamchimjil* or *homjil* (you will be stitching through four layers of fabric).

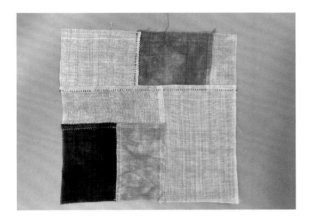
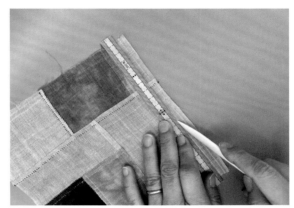

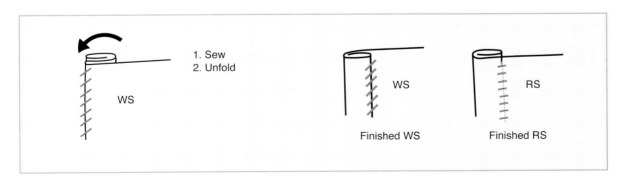

Decorative motifs

Jatssi, Jatmulligi, Jatmulim (잣씨, 잣물리기, 잣물림): Pine nut

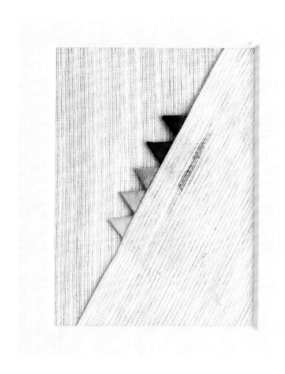

A small square piece of fabric is used to make a tiny triangular decorative motif called *jatssi*.

Clusters of multiple color *jatssi* are used to decorate corners and edges, or are stitched on to the seam lines of bojagi or *hanbok*.

1. Start with a piece of fabric, approximately ½" [12 mm] square.

2. Fold the fabric along the diagonal to make an upside-down triangle shape and pinch the triangle in the middle to mark the center.

3. Take the left side and fold toward the middle, past the bottom point. Then fold the other side to the middle to make a top angle of 60 degrees.

4. Baste/tack with an X to keep the folds.

5. Make additional triangles in different colors. Slightly overlap them and baste them together.

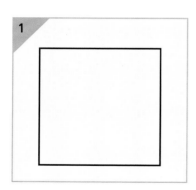
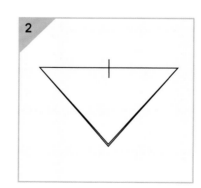

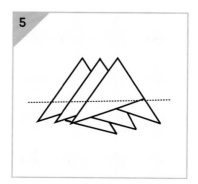

Bakjwi maedeup (박쥐 매듭): Bat-shaped knot

Bakjwi maedeup is a tiny, rolled fabric decoration that resembles an open-winged bat.

In Korean culture, bats are considered a symbol of happiness, as the character for bat (蝠, 복) and the character for happiness (福, 복) are homophones. *Bakjwi maedeup* is made and sewn on to bojagi to obtain happiness. However, *bakjwi maedeup* can also be used as a decorative design element and for securing more than two layers of fabric together.

1. Prepare a 15" [38 cm] double thread with a knot, and a piece of fabric 2" [5 cm] square. Place two pins diagonally in opposite corners of the square of fabric.

2. Roll the pinned corners toward the center, one at a time, until the two meet in the center.

3. Take the pins out and fold the rolled part in half. Use clip(s) or your fingers to hold it in place.

4. Stitch through the rolled part, ¼" [6 mm] from the top from the fold, to secure the shape. Turn the rolled part over to stitch the other side. Repeat stitching. Wrap and tie thread around the stitched part.

5. Trim off the bottom part but leave thread attached to the shape. Put glue on the cut edge to prevent fraying. In Korea, in the old days, one grain of cooked rice was applied instead of glue.

6. Place your index finger under the cut edge to support and gently pull open two rolled parts from the top with both thumbs to get the *bakjwi* shape. Sew the *bakjwi maedeup* on the bojagi by stitching through to the bojagi and stitching back up and down. Make two sets of tiny stitches near each wing to secure *bakjwi maedeup* firmly.

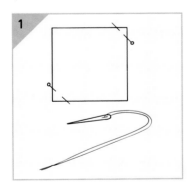
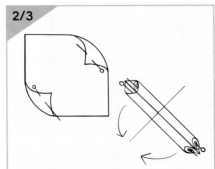
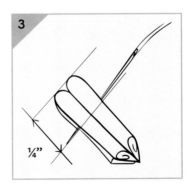
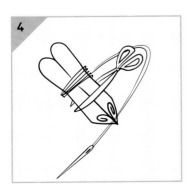
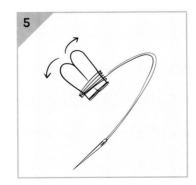

Yeouijumun (여의주문): Wish-fulfilling jewel or cathedral window pattern

1. Cut a 5" [12.5 cm] square piece of fabric and score ¼" [6 mm] seam allowances on all four sides. Fold and iron the creased lines to the wrong side.

2. Mark the center point by creasing and folding diagonally and horizontally.

3. Thread a needle with a single thread and make a knot at the end.

4. Pull the needle through the center mark from the back of the fabric **(a)**.

5. Go through the four corners and pull the needle and thread to the center **(b)**.

6. Put the needle and thread through the center point to the back and iron the folded lines **(c)**.

7. Turn upside-down and put the needle through the four corners again. Put the needle through to the back and tie a knot. Now the square is 2¼" [5.7 cm] **(d and e)**.

8. Make another unit using steps 1–7.

9. Connect the two units using *gamchimjil* **(f)**.

10. Repeat until you have four connected units.

Cut a 1⅜" [3.5 cm] square of contrasting fabric. Trim off all four sides to get a curved line. Place the fabric in the middle of the stitched units and baste it. Gently fold the four surrounding bias edges toward the center square.

11. Stitch on the folded edges using *homjil* (running stitch) or *ban bageumjil* (half back stitch). Five to six stitches on each side would be ideal. Now you have a finished four-piece *yeouijumun* block (see p.116).

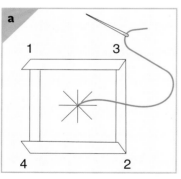

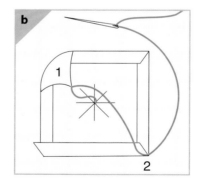

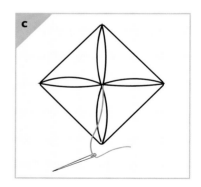

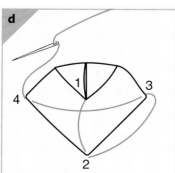

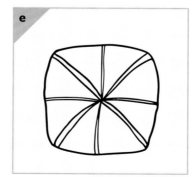

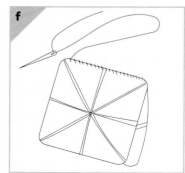

Dorae maedeup: Double crossed knot

1. Fold the cord in half and hold both sides of the cord together with your left hand.

2. Take the A cord (the one closest to your body) and place it away from you, making a loop that crosses over the B cord.

3. Put the end of the A cord through the loop you just made.

4. Using your right thumb, push only the loop away from you until it comes back up around the bottom.

5. Hold in place with your left hand. Make a new loop with the B cord right next to the first loop.

6. Put the end of the B cord through both loops.

7. Holding the bottom of both loops with your left hand, slowly pull the A cord until the knot is snug and you can see where it crosses over itself.

8. Pull the B cord slowly, and cover that crossed part with the cord as it tightens.

9. Now you can see crossed cords in both the front and the back.

You can find a tutorial to help you on my website: www.youngminlee.com/video/602

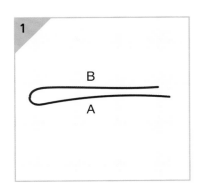

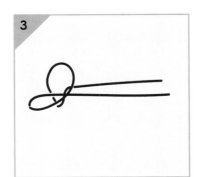

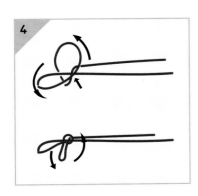

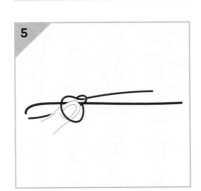

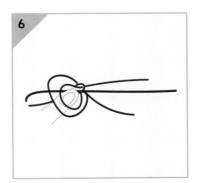

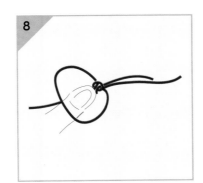

Yeonbong maedeup (연봉 매듭): Lotus bud knot

1. Fold the cord in half and place the middle point on top of your left index finger. The half hanging down in front should be to the left (left cord), and the half hanging down behind your finger should be to the right (right cord).

2. Place your right index finger behind the right cord. Pull the right cord down and toward you while twisting, to make a loop. Hold in place with your left thumb.

3. Take the left cord and place it behind the free end of the right cord. Put the left cord through the right cord loop you made in step 2, going from the front to the back. Then place the right cord to the left, pulling it between the cord and your left index finger.

4. Still using the right cord, bring it back to the right and go through the same loop as step 3, this time from back to front.

5. Place the end of the right cord up near your left index finger. The crossed cords should resemble a figure 8, with a small diamond shape in the middle.

6. Keep the cord shape on your left index finger and turn your hand over so you can see the back of your hand. Slide your left index finger out from the cord shape. Now you should see a top loop with the figure 8 underneath. Take the end of the cord at the top of the shape. Moving clockwise, go around the bottom part of the top loop, and place the cord into the diamond shape in the middle.

7. Take the end of the cord at the bottom of the shape. Moving clockwise, go around the top part of the top loop, and place the cord into the diamond shape in the middle as before.

8. Hold the top loop in your left hand, and the two cords on the other side in your right hand. Gently pull both the loop and the two ends, until the shape in the middle turns into a *yeonbong* shape.

A tutorial to help you can be found on my website: www.youngminlee.com/video/9469

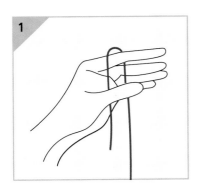

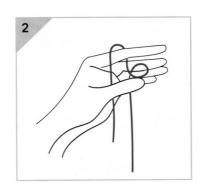

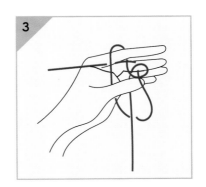

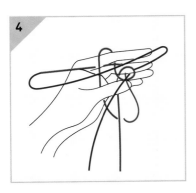

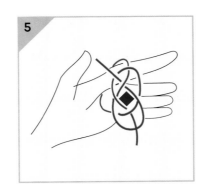

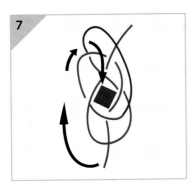

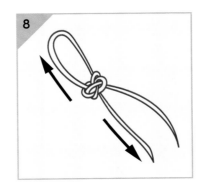

7
Before You Start

How to tie a knot

This is a very neat way to make a knot before you start to stitch. I don't remember who taught me this method, but it must have been my mother or grandmother. For as long as I can remember, whenever I begin to make something with hand stitching, I use this method. You can make a knot at the very end of the thread, controlling the size of the knot with the number of times you wrap the thread around the needle. I usually work with a single thread, making a knot on one end and keeping the other end shorter while I stitch. A comfortable length of thread for me is approximately the length of my forearm. I cut a piece of thread approximately 16" [40 cm] long. This length allows me to manage my sewing without getting knots, twists or tangles.

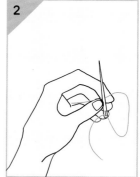
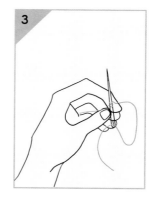

Let's tie a starting knot:

1. Thread the needle and hold the long end of the thread between your left thumb and index finger, with the longer thread tail trailing to the left.

2. Place a needle on top of the thread to make a cross shape with the thread and the needle.

3. Using the thread on the right side of the needle, wrap the thread around the needle 2–3 times. If you want to make a bigger knot, wrap the thread a few more times.

4. Hold the wraps with your left thumb and index finger and pull out the needle gently with your right hand. Keep a firm hold on the needle until you feel the knot in between your fingers.

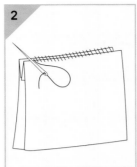

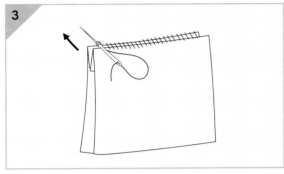

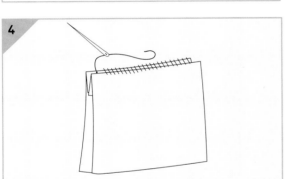

Now we'll make an ending knot:

1. When you reach the end of your sewing, take the last stitch into the back layer of fabric only and bring the needle out between the two layers (i.e. the front and back layers of fabric).

2. Place the needle right on top of the thread, with the needle pointing towards the back layer of fabric.

3. Wrap the thread around the needle 2–3 times and firmly hold the wraps with the left thumb and index finger.

4. Gently pull the needle all the way through the wraps, until you feel the knot in between your fingers.

5. Take the needle through the front layer of fabric to bury the knot.

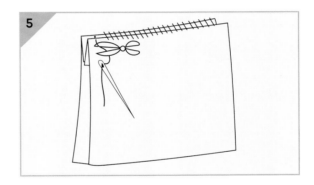

Projects

Some projects have precise measurements, and some don't have many measurements except for seam allowances. Designing bojagi, especially *jogakbo*, is a very intuitive process that happens while you're making, so please don't worry when you don't see predetermined measurements or finished sizes. I hope you will enjoy the process with fewer rules, and find joy in adding your own ideas, color choices and design decisions – and, hopefully, you will find your own happiness while you stitch.

Seam allowances

- For the most part, seam allowances are ¼" [6 mm].
- *Ssamsol* needs two different seam allowances: ¼" [6 mm] and ½" [12 mm].
- Some larger projects like window coverings and four-point cushions need ½" [12 mm] seam allowances for double-fold hems or piecing.

Ssamsol 101

On p.52 I outlined the basic *ssamsol* technique, which used two *gamchimjil*. In this section I will go into more detail about how to work this technique, and how to use it to construct larger *jogakgo* pieces.

There are four variations of *ssamsol* but they all follow one rule: two different seam allowances, where one seam allowance is twice as wide as the other one so it can cover the narrower seam allowance. These four variations will show slightly different combinations of stitch techniques:

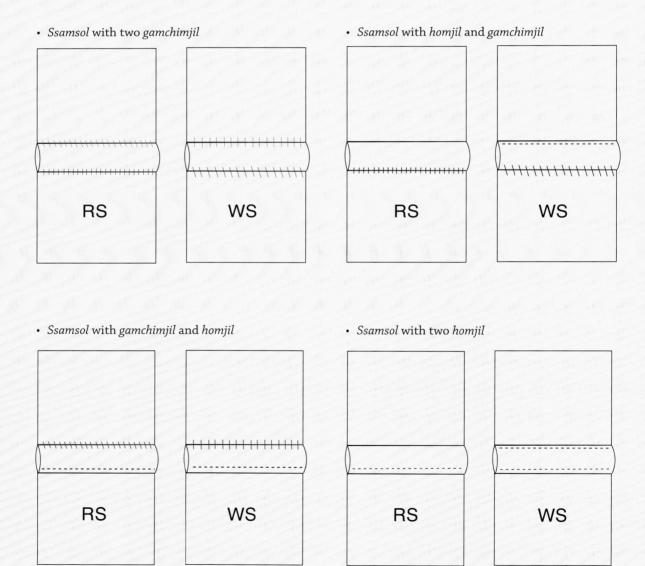

- *Ssamsol* with two *gamchimjil*

- *Ssamsol* with *homjil* and *gamchimjil*

- *Ssamsol* with *gamchimjil* and *homjil*

- *Ssamsol* with two *homjil*

Using different types of ssamsol to create larger pieces

Straight line ssamsol

1. Prepare fabric pieces with two different seam allowances. One seam allowance should be twice the width of the other, so it can cover the smaller seam allowance.

2. Make a removable/erasable mark on the right side of the first fabric (I usually mark with French knots). Then using a bone folder, score a double seam allowance (DSA) on one short edge. Fold down the DSA from the right side of the fabric to the wrong side of the fabric.

3. Take the second piece of fabric and score a regular seam allowance (RSA) on one short edge of the right side of the fabric. Fold down the RSA from the right side of the fabric to the wrong side of the fabric.

4. Place the folded seam allowances together and sew with *gamchimjil* (whip stitch) from the right side, making evenly sized slanted stitch marks on the right side of the fabric.

5. Press to open the seam.

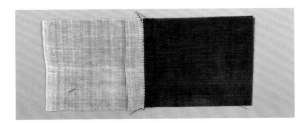

6. Move the bigger seam allowance over toward the smaller seam allowance to cover the edge.

7. Score a line in the middle of the bigger seam allowance, and fold down along the crease to cover the smaller seam allowance.

8. Score another line right at the edge of the folded bigger seam allowance, and fold the back fabric so you have two folded parts.

9. Sew another line with *gamchimjil* at the edge of these two folds.

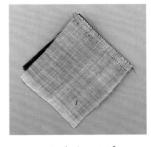

10. Unfold and press the two connected pieces of fabrics. Now you are done with your first *ssamsol*!

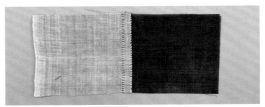

Slanted or angled *ssamsol*

1. Prepare two pieces of fabric.

2. With right sides facing up, place the left fabric on top of the right one and make sure that they overlap by at least 2" [5 cm].

3. You want to make sure that there is at least ½" [12 mm] seam allowance along the entire slanted line. Mark a slanted line with fabric marker on the top layer.

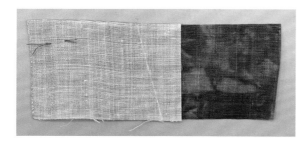

4. With a ruler on top of the two layers of fabric, score the marked line (marking both the top and the bottom layers). Fold under both seam allowances from the right side to the wrong side of the fabric.

5. Place the folded seam allowances together and sew with *gamchimjil* from the right side.

6. Open the seam, press, and trim the seam allowances: one with ½" [12 mm] and the other with ¼" [6 mm] (a ratio of 2:1 applies when you use different size seam allowances).

7. Fold the larger seam allowance down toward the smaller seam allowance to cover its edge. Score a line in the middle of the bigger seam.

8. Fold down using the crease to cover the smaller seam.

9. Score another line right at the edge of the folded larger seam, and fold the back fabric so you can see two folded edges.

10. Sew another line with *gamchimjil* at the edge of these two folds and press.

11. Unfold and press down the two connected pieces of fabrics.

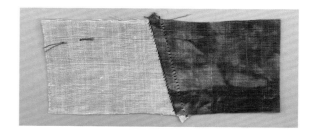

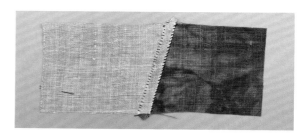

Block construction method

You can add new pieces, either horizontally or vertically, to make your desired size of fabric. Then you can connect the strips together or build your *jogakbo* in a spiral outward as you make a log cabin quilt block.

1. Cut and prepare a new piece of fabric with a regular seam allowance.

2. Add on the side of the previous piece. Make sure to give a double seam allowance on the right side of #2 piece (this is a piece without a French knot mark) and from the right side (top to bottom) and connect the new piece, #3, with a regular seam allowance.

3. To add pieces horizontally, the seam allowance should be on the left/right edge.

4. To add pieces vertically, the seam allowance should be on the top/bottom edge.

5. Continue to work in a spiral, connecting pieces in the same manner. Now you can build your block and make your *ssamsol jogakbo* grow.

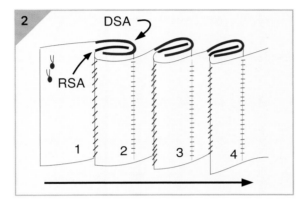

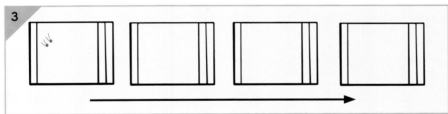

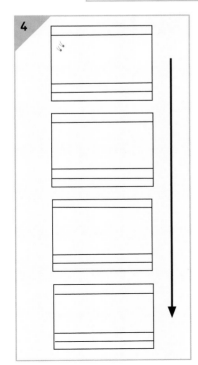

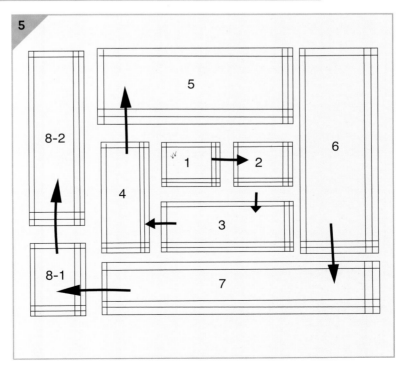

Flower Pincushion (*Oyat Kkot*)

Oyat kkot (plum blossom) is a symbol of the Korean Empire (1897–1910), and my maiden name, Lee (이, 李), means 'plum tree' in Chinese script. The last time I went to Korea, I visited a number of museums – I saw many artifacts decorated with *oyat kkot*, and fell in love with this simple, elegant flower.

To make this pincushion, I used naturally dyed linen fabric and wool stuffing. The fabric came from Kristine and Adrienne, the dynamic duo behind A Verb for Keeping Warm – a lovely studio and shop in Oakland, California. They dye beautiful fabrics and yarns with natural dyestuffs. Weld and fustic created the yellow, and the fabric that looks like it's been sprinkled with confetti was dyed with marigold petals.

FINISHED SIZE

Circumference: 3½" [9 cm]
Height: 1¾" [4.5 cm]

MATERIALS

I used naturally dyed, lightweight linen for this project. *Myeongju* (plain weave Korean silk) is another material I use a lot of the time. You can try with lightweight or medium-weight plain weave materials of your choice.

    You will need:
    2¼" [5.7 cm] squares x 5
    2¼ x 2¾" [5.7 x 7 cm] rectangles x 5
    2" [5 cm] square (for the *bakjwi maedeup*) x 1
    4" [10 cm] square to cover a round piece of cardboard for the base x 1
    2½" [6.4 cm] diameter round piece of cardboard x 1
    Stuffing: wool or polyester
    Cotton thread
    Needle

Stitches used

Gamchimjil (whip stitch) – see p.44.
Sichimjil (basting stitch) – see p.44.

INSTRUCTIONS

1. On all 5 squares and 5 rectangles, mark, fold, and press a ¼" [6 mm] seam allowance on all sides **(a)**.

2. Whip stitch squares together, leaving the seam allowance unstitched. Pieces should form a star shape **(b)**.

3. Whip stitch short sides of rectangles to sides of squares **(c)**.

4. Whip stitch long sides of rectangles to edges of adjacent squares/rectangles **(d)**.

5. Baste stitch around the open bottom of the pincushion **(e)**.

6. Fill pincushion with stuffing. Pull basting stitches tight and knot the thread **(f)**.

7. Stitch down each of the 5 outer-most corners of the squares **(g)**.

8. Pull thread tight to pull corners down/into pincushion **(h)**.

9. Stitch down the top center 5 times, making sure to pull the thread tight each time **(i)**.

10. Make *bakjwi maedeup* (bat-shaped knot, see p.55) and attach to the center of the pincushion. You can also make a loose tassel bunch to attach to the center, as shown on p.70.

11. To make the bottom, place the 4" [10 cm] square of fabric on the cardboard circle, right side up. Baste stitch corners and pull tight **(j)**.

12. Place against bottom of pincushion, right side out, and whip stitch together **(k)**.

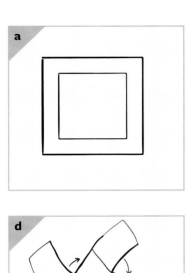

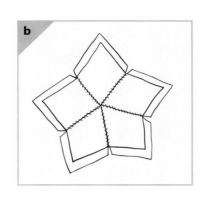

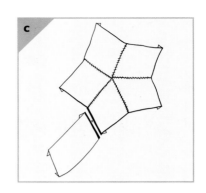

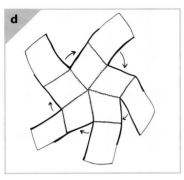

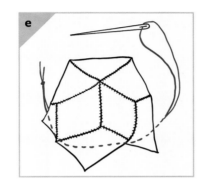

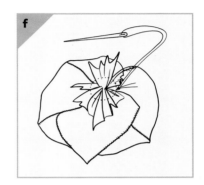

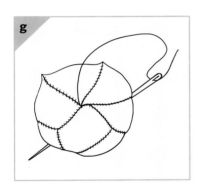

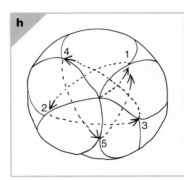

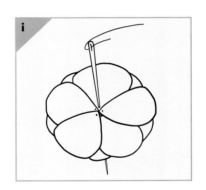

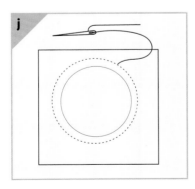

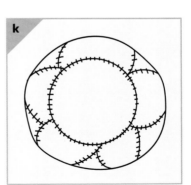

HOW TO MAKE A TASSEL OR A LOOSE TASSEL BUNCH

1. Cut out a 2 x 3" [5 x 7.5 cm] piece of cardboard and wrap thread around it 30 times **(a)**.

2. Remove the wrapped thread from the cardboard, wrap a thread 2–3 times around the center and tie a knot **(b)**.

3. Fold it in half, wrap around 2–3 times on the top fold and tie a knot to secure the shape **(c)**.

4. If you want a tassel, trim the end and place the wrapped middle section into the center of the pincushion and secure it. If you want to finish as a loose tassel bunch, don't trim, but just attach to the pincushion as for the tassel **(d)**.

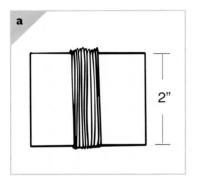

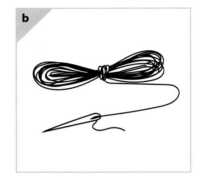

Lotus Leaf Mat
(*Yeonnip*)

One summer, my friend Sara came to visit from England. She stayed for a week at my house to learn bojagi techniques with me. After teaching her numerous hand stitching techniques during the day, late afternoon tea in my garden was a wonderful way to wind down and wrap up the busy day.

Ever since then, I've developed a habit of having a cup of tea (sometimes, a cup of coffee) in the afternoon. I boil water and set my small teapot and a cup on my lotus leaf mat, and I am ready to enjoy a quiet, relaxing time to recharge myself. The lotus is a symbol of purity, enlightenment, and rebirth in many cultures.

FINISHED SIZE

Width: 15" [38 cm]
Length: 12" [30 cm]

MATERIALS

- 1 yard [90 cm] *mosi* (ramie) or ½ yard [45 cm] linen
- Bias tape maker
- Painter's tape
- Cotton sewing thread
- Hand-sewing needle
- Lotus leaf mat template (see pp.150–154)

Stitches used

Homjil (running stitch) – see p.43.
Gamchimjil (whip stitch) – see p.44.
Kkojipgi (pin tuck stitch) – see p.48.

INSTRUCTIONS

1. Cut ½ yard [45 cm] *mosi* fabric. Note: *mosi* comes in a narrow width between 12–14" [30–35 cm], so ½ yard [45 cm] will be approximately 12 x 18" [30 x 45 cm].

2. Place the pattern under the fabric and put painter's tape on each corner to prevent it from shifting.

3. Using a fabric pencil, trace the pattern on the fabric.

4. Using a bone folder, mark leaf veins **(a)**.

5. Pinch those marked leaf veins with fingers to make raised lines **(b)**.

6. Press with iron on the pinch marked lines.

7. *Homjil* along the pinched lines. This technique is called *kkojipgi* in bojagi making **(c)**.

8. Trim along the outline of the pattern. Fold a ¼" [6 mm] hem allowance twice **(d)**.

9. *Gamchimjil* to finish **(e)**.

10. Cut a 1 x 15" [2.5 x 38 cm] piece of fabric at a 45 degree angle to make bias tape.

11. Using a ½" [12 mm] bias tape maker, iron and make ¼" [6 mm] double-fold bias tape.

12. *Homjil* along the folded line.

13. Make a *yeonbong maedeup* (lotus bud knot, see p.58).

14. Attach the *yeonbong maedeup* by stitching it to the center of the lotus leaf mat **(f)**.

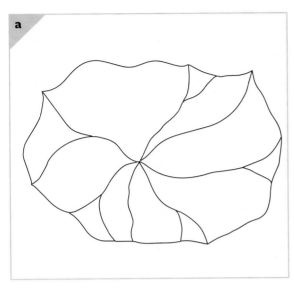

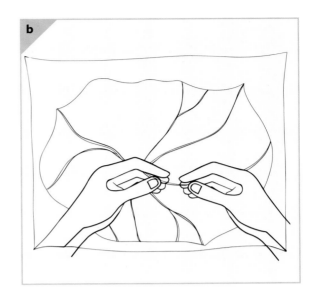

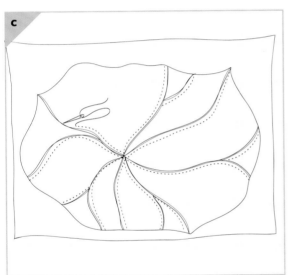

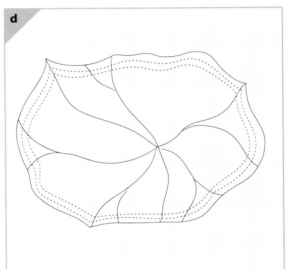

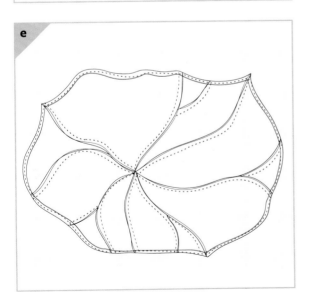

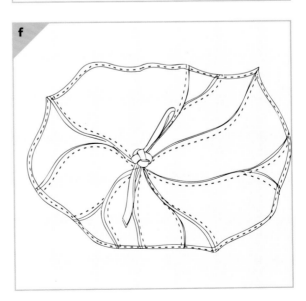

Four-Point Cushion
(*Nemo Bangseok*)

Hand sewing is a meditative practice for me. I 'wish happiness' while I sew, imbuing my stitched pieces with good luck and positive thoughts. This project is a cascade of squares sewn into a four-point cushion. I hope that you can wish for happiness while you work!

FINISHED SIZE

Large cushion
Diameter: 12" [30 cm]
Height: 7½" [19 cm]

Small cushion
Diameter: 5½" [14 cm]
Height: 4" [10 cm]

MATERIALS

Large cushion
½ yard [45 cm] of 1¼ yard [1.1 m] wide solid cotton or linen

Small cushion
¼ yard [23 cm] of 1¼ yard [1.1 m] wide solid cotton or linen

Both cushions
- Several lengths of cotton or linen scraps to make patchwork squares
- 40wt or 50wt cotton thread
- Sewing needle
- Long sashiko needle for making and attaching *bakjwi maedeup* (bat-shaped knot)
- 2 long pins (1¾" [4.5 cm] long) or 2 long basting needles for making *bakjwi maedeup*
- Wool stuffing or polyester fiberfill

Stitches used
Gamchimjil (whip stitch) – see p.44.

Notes
This project uses ½" [12 mm] seam allowances throughout. The illustrations use the measurements for the large cushion size. The small cushion size uses the same seam allowance width, smaller squares, and is sewn the same way.

INSTRUCTIONS

Before you start, cut fabric for solid squares as follows:

Large cushion:

7" [18 cm] squares of solid cotton or linen x 8
2" [5 cm] squares of cotton fabric (for *bakjwi maedeup*) x 2

Small cushion:

4" [10 cm] squares of solid cotton or linen x 8
4" [10 cm] patchwork squares made of cotton or linen scraps x 4
2" [5 cm] squares of cotton fabric (for *bakjwi maedeup*) x 2

1. Make patchwork squares (*jogakbo*): using a ½" [12 mm] seam allowance and *gamchimjil*, sew small scraps of fabric together. Make a 7" [18 cm] square for large cushion (or 4" [10 cm] for small cushion), sewing all the way to the edge of the piece. Make 4 of these patchwork squares **(a)**.

2. Using two solid linen squares and one patchwork square, *gamchimjil* the three squares together to make an alternating strip: solid, patchwork, solid, with the patchwork square in the middle. Stop and start ½" [12 mm] from the edges, leaving the seam allowance on the sides unsewn. Make four of these strips **(b)**.

3. *Gamchimjil* the four strips together. Stagger them **(c)**, making sure to stop and start ½" [12 mm] from the raw outer edges. Make a

note of the * and ** placement.

4. Once the four strips are sewn together, there will be two patchwork pieces with free edges. The sides marked * connect to each other, and the sides marked ** connect to each other. Sew these together, using a ½" [12 mm] seam allowance and *gamchimjil*.

5. *Gamchimjil* each free edge of the solid color squares to the adjacent solid color free edge. This time, sew across the seam allowances to

the edge of the fabric. Leave one small opening **(d, e** and **f)**.

6. Stuff with filling. *Gamchimjil* the opening closed **(g** and **h)**.

7. Attach one *bakjwi maedeup* in the center on the top of the cushion, and another on the bottom. Bring the needle and thread all the way through the cushion, to pinch it slightly in the center **(i)**.

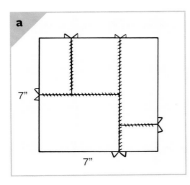

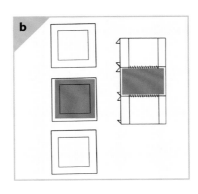

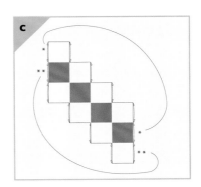

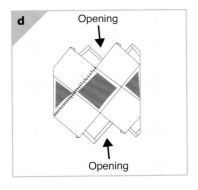

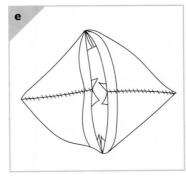

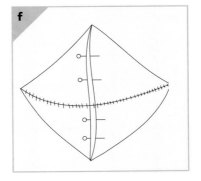

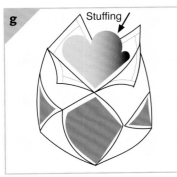

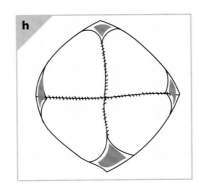

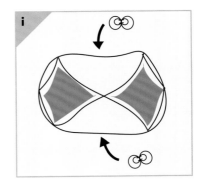

Gift-wrap Bojagi (*Yemulbo*)

Neatly wrapped gifts make me smile, whether they are given or received. *Yemul*, a precious object or gift for special occasions such as weddings, is wrapped in bojagi. Sometimes auspicious symbols and patterns are embroidered on the fabrics, or solid color fabrics are used. The *yemulbo* that I received from my mother-in-law on my wedding day is one of the most precious bojagi that I have.

Think about making a bojagi and wrapping a gift with it. You add your love and send it with your gift. When I make *yemulbo*, I often use *sukgosa* (traditional Korean silk gauze), but you can use different materials. Once I played with combining my own tea-dyed silk organza, onion-skin-dyed cotton, and printed Liberty London Tana Lawn cotton. Sheer or translucent materials and small-patterned fabrics work well together.

FINISHED SIZE

Width: 13" [33 cm]
Length: 13" [33 cm]

MATERIALS

- Assorted fabric scraps to make a 5 x 7" [12.5 x 18 cm] patchwork piece (A)
- *Sukgosa* (patterned Korean silk), or your choice of fabric
  You will need:
  5 x 7" [12.5 x 18 cm] solid piece x 1 (B)
  9 x 13½" [23 x 34 cm] solid piece x 1 (C)
  13½ x 13½" [34 x 34 cm] solid piece x 1 (D)
  2½ x 26" [6.4 x 66 cm] (for the strap) x 1 (E)
- Silk thread
- Needle

Stitches used

Gamchimjil (whip stitch) – see p.44.
Settam sangchim (decorative triple stitch) – see p.46.

Notes

¼" [6 mm] seam allowances on all sides are included in the measurements above. Press all seam allowances toward wrong sides before sewing.

INSTRUCTIONS

1. Put together your patchwork (*jogakbo*) design: place two small pieces of your choice, folded seam allowances together, stitch on the right side of the fabric using *gamchimjil*. Add more pieces until you have a 5 x 7" [12.5 x 18 cm] patchwork piece. This is piece A.

2. Sew short sides of pieces A and B together using *gamchimjil*.

3. Sew long side of this piece to long side of C using *gamchimjil* with right sides facing out. This is now the front piece **(a)**.

4. Sew front piece to D (back piece) along all four sides using *gamchimjil* with right sides facing out **(b)**.

5. Fold piece E in half lengthwise, right side facing out **(c)**.

6. *Gamchimjil* all three open sides closed, starting at the folded corner of one short side **(d)**.

7. Attach E to the outer corner of piece A (your patchwork block) using *settam sangchim* **(e** and **f)**.

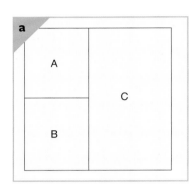

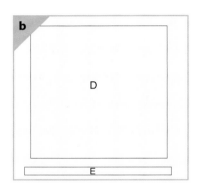

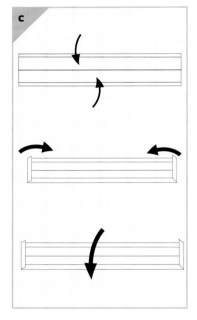

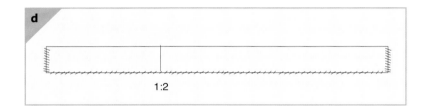

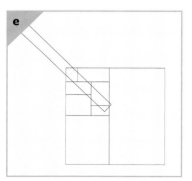

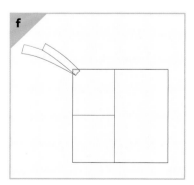

BOJAGI: The Art of Korean Textiles

How to fold *yemulbo* and tie *goreum* (one bow sash)

When you finish making your *yemulbo*, you might want to know how to wrap a gift or letter. Let's do it together.

1. Place your *yemulbo* right side down, and make sure the corner with straps is at the top. Place your item (either a gift or a letter) in the center of the *yemulbo* **(a)**.

2. Fold the bottom corner up toward the center, partially covering your item. Tuck the corner down behind your item **(b)**.

3. Fold the left side toward the center, then fold the right side toward the center. Your item should be mostly or fully covered **(c)**.

4. Fold the bottom toward the top once, then fold the top corner with straps down **(d** and **e)**.

5. Wrap the long strap once around the wrapped *yemulbo*. Now you have two straps on the top of the wrapped part **(f)**.

6. Place the shorter strap over the longer one. Wrap the short strap around the long one so that the two straps are crossed **(g)**.

7. Fold the long strap about 2" [5 cm] from where they are crossed, to make a half of a bow shape **(h)**.

8. Wrap the short strap around that folded part and pull it through behind the folded straps **(i)**.

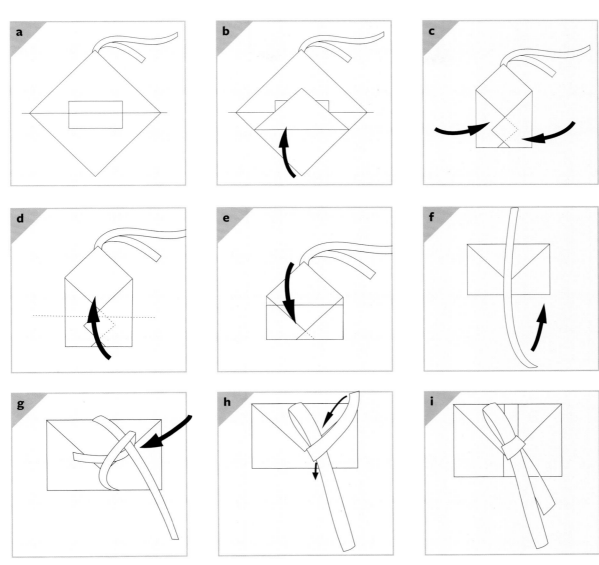

Covering Bojagi (Sangbo)

When I was young, coming back home after a long day at school and finding my mother's neatly and affectionately arranged rice cakes and fruit, covered by a *sangbo*, made me happy. Using four panels of fabrics and *ssamsol* technique, you can make this simple *sangbo* to cover your food tray or tea set.

FINISHED SIZE

Width: 15" [38 cm]
Length: 15" [38 cm]

MATERIALS

- *Mosi* (ramie)
  You will need:
  1 yard [90 cm] for *sangbo*
  ¼ yard [22.5 cm] for *yeongwi* (corner decorations) x 4
  and *bakjwi maedeup* x 3
- Cotton thread
- Needle
- Covering bojagi template (p.156)

Stitches used

Homjil (running stitch) – see p.43.
Gamchimjil (whip stitch) – see p.44.
Ssamsol (flat felled seam) – see p.52.

Notes

This project uses ¼" [6 mm] and ½" [12 mm] seam allowances.

INSTRUCTIONS

1. Cut fabrics as follows:

8½" [22 cm] square x 1 (A)
8¼ x 8½" [21 x 22 cm] rectangle x 2 (B and C)
8¼" [21 cm] square x 1 (D)

2. Mark seam allowances as shown **(a)**.

3. Sew A and B together with *ssamsol* technique.

4. Sew C and D together with *ssamsol* technique.

5. Connect these two pieces together with *ssamsol* technique.

6. For the double-fold hem (see p.53), fold the hem allowance to the wrong side of the fabric twice.

7. Score at the fold line, and fold toward the right side.

8. Secure the hem using *gamchimjil* or *homjil* (you will be stitching through four layers of fabric).

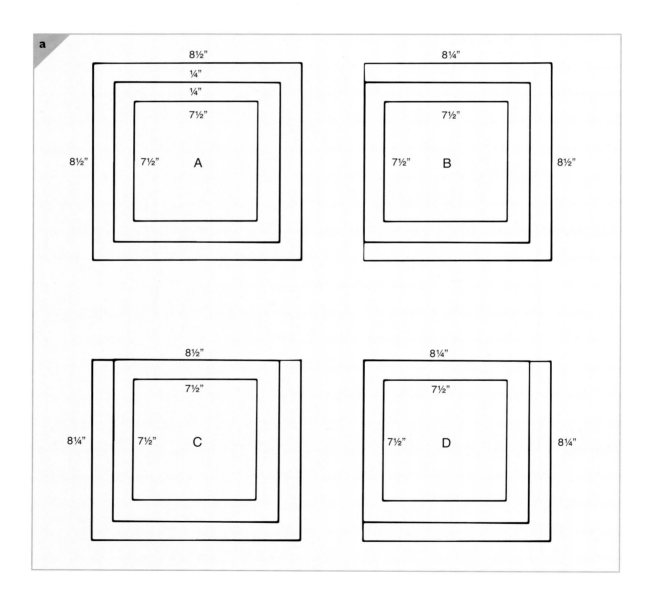

Making corner decorations (*yeongwi*)

1. Trace covering bojagi template (p.156) onto cardboard and cut out the shape.

2. Use the cardboard template to trace the shape onto the fabric and cut out four shapes.

3. Using the cardboard template, fold seam allowance toward the shape. If necessary, snip the convex part of the seam allowance so the curve can fold smoothly.

4. Shape these curves with your hands and an iron to hold the lines. Place a *yeongwi* shape on each corner of the square bojagi and attach with *gamchimjil*. Start from one corner of the shape, then move to the curves and back down to the corner again.

Knob with *bakjwi maedeup*

1. Cut a 2½ x 6½" [6.4 x 16.5 cm] piece of fabric.

2. Mark a ¼" [6 mm] seam allowance around four edges.

3. Place the wrong side up, fold the long side seam allowances toward the wrong side **(b)**.

4. Fold the short side seam allowances toward the wrong side **(c)**.

5. Fold the fabric in half lengthwise, right side facing out **(d)**.

6. Press and sew three open sides with *gamchimjil*. Fold the long side of the strip in half, so the two ends meet **(e)**.

7. Make three *bakjwi maedeup* (see p.55) and attach side by side below the fold **(f)**.

8. Sew this knob with the three *bakjwi maedeup* on the center of the *sangbo*.

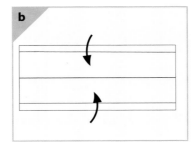

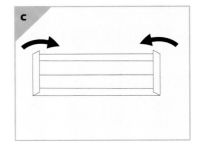

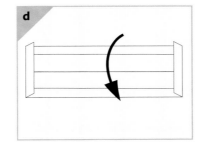

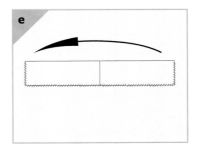

Flower-Shaped Pouch
(*Kkot Jumeoni*)

This simple yet versatile *jumeoni* (pouch) is very easy to make. When you are not using it, you can store it in its flat form. When you put something inside, it becomes a three-dimensional shape. The four petals and finished shape remind me of the persimmon flowers that I played with in my childhood.

FINISHED SIZE

Width: 12" [30 cm]
Length: 12" [30 cm]

MATERIALS

- 12½" [32 cm] square of *saekdong* silk or *sukgosa* x 2
- 1 yard [90 cm] cord or ribbon of your choice x 2
- Silk thread
- Needle

Stitches used
Homjil (running stitch) – see p.43.
Gonggeureugi (blind stitch) – see p.47.

Notes
This project uses a seam allowance of ¼" [6 mm] throughout.

INSTRUCTIONS

1. Take your two squares of fabric and stitch around the edges with *homjil*, then turn inside out **(a)**.

2. Close the opening with *gonggeureugi*.

3. Fold four corners into center **(b)**.

4. From each corner, fold the tip to the outside edge **(c)**.

5. Mark ½" [12 mm] from the new fold and stitch two layers together to make casings **(d)**.

6. Insert two cords and tie two neighboring cords together (AB, CD) **(e)**.

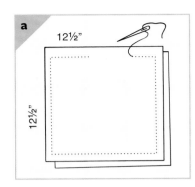

a

12½"

12½"

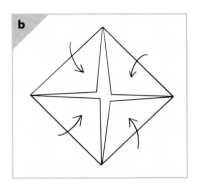

b

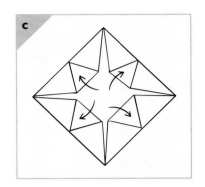

c

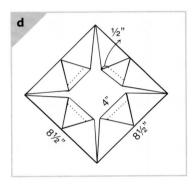

d

½"

4"

8½"   8½"

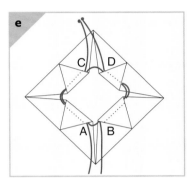

e

C   D

A   B

Jogakbo-Style Placemat

Mosi (ramie) is a very practical and durable material that is easy to wash and use in daily life. Subtle pastel colors of ramie brighten my mealtimes. This is a good project to practice *ssamsol* technique.

FINISHED SIZE

Width: 12½" [32 cm]
Length: 18" [46 cm]

MATERIALS

- 5 x 2" [12.5 x 5 cm] or 5 x 3" [12.5 x 7.5 cm] pieces of ramie (various colors) x 5 or 6
- 12½ x 15" [32 x 38 cm] piece of ramie
- Silk thread
- Needle

Stitches used
Ssamsol (flat felled seam) – see p.52.

Notes
I used the whole width of ramie, so I didn't worry about finishing the edges with double folds. If you are using wider width fabrics and cutting them to size, then add a ½" [12 mm] seam allowance for a double-fold hem (see p.53).

INSTRUCTIONS

1. Using small ramie pieces in various colors and *ssamsol* technique, make one 5 x 13½" [12.5 x 34 cm] strip **(a)**.

2. Finish the two 5" [12.5 cm] ends of the pieced block with double-fold hems (see p. 53).

3. Using *ssamsol*, connect the large piece of ramie and the pieced block **(b)**.

4. Finish the two side ends 12½" [32 cm] with double-fold hems.

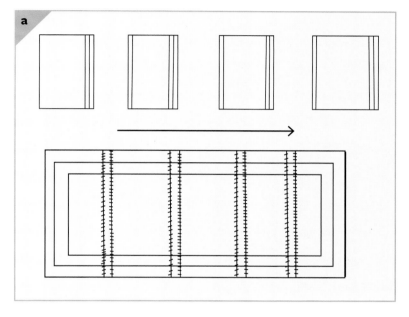

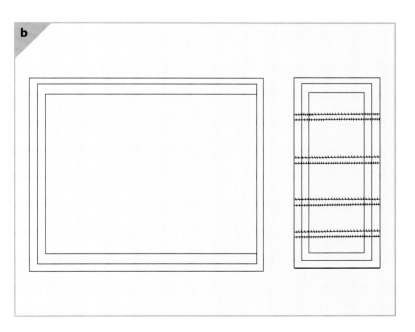

Jogakbo Tote Bag

I have spent some time practicing dyeing fabrics in my backyard. As a result, I have accumulated many colors and hues of linen, cotton and wool fabrics. My fabrics are not perfectly dyed, but I enjoy the imperfect and unexpected results of my own work. I put small pieces of fabric together using the *ssamsol* technique that I often use when I make *jogakbo*. I have a finished size in mind for the piece of fabric, but the design grows as I connect pieces together. This organic process always brings me joy. I made one tote with fabric handles and another with leather handles. There are instructions for both versions here.

FINISHED SIZE

Width: approximately 18" [46 cm]
Length: 14" [36 cm]
Depth: 6" [15 cm]
Handle: 22" [56 cm]

MATERIALS

- 1 x 1½ yard [90 x 140 cm] medium-weight linen
  (I cut it into four pieces and dyed different shades with madder)
- 1 x 1¼ yard [90 x 110 cm] muslin
- 1 yard [90 cm] fusible interfacing (such as Pellon SF101)
- Matching sewing thread: 40wt cotton or polyester sewing thread for *bageumjil* or *ban bageumjil* on bottom triangle sections

Fabric handle option
Trigger snap o-ring 1⅜"
[3.5 cm] x 2

Leather handle option
Trigger snap o-ring 1⅜" [3.5 cm] x 6
14¼" [36.2 cm] leather handle with trigger snap o-ring 1⅜" [3.5 cm] x 2

Stitches used
Ssamsol (flat felled seam) – see p.52.
Bageumjil (back stitch) – see p.45.
Ban bageumjil (half back stitch) – see p.46.
Sangchim (top stitch) – see p.46.

Notes
This project uses a ½" [12 mm] seam allowance throughout, which is included in all measurements except the fabric handle.

INSTRUCTIONS

Exterior

1. Using *ssamsol*, make a patchwork piece 19" [48 cm] wide and 35" [89 cm] long. This will be folded in half to make the exterior of the tote. You can patchwork the entire piece, or just piece 19 x 14" [48 x 36 cm], with a solid color for the rest **(a)**.

2. Place the right side of the fabric face down, and apply the bumpy side of the fusible interfacing down on the wrong side of the fabric piece.

3. Cover with a damp ironing cloth and iron until the fusible interfacing is stuck to the fabric.

4. Face the right sides of the fabric together and fold in half lengthwise.

5. Sew on both side seam lines. Open the seam and press with an iron.

6. Turn right side out.

7. Mark a 3" [7.5 cm] square on each side of the base with a fabric marker.

8. Pinch the bottom corners, to align the side seam on top of the centerline of the bottom.

9. *Bageumjil* or *ban bageumjil* on the marked lines. Now you will see a pointed triangle on each side **(b)**.

Lining and pocket

1. Cut a 19" [48 cm] wide, 35" [89 cm] long piece of muslin.

2. Cut a piece of linen 11" [28 cm] wide and 12" [31 cm] long. Face the right sides together and fold in half lengthwise.

3. Sew around the edges with a ½" [12 mm] seam allowance. Leave a 2" [5 cm] gap on one side and turn inside out, and iron **(c)**.

4. Top stitch along one long side of the pocket. This will be the top part of the pocket **(d)**.

5. Place the pocket 5½" [14 cm] from the top of the lining fabric on the right side and sew **(e)**.

6. With right sides together, fold the lining in half. Sew both side seams.

7. Mark 3½ x 3" [9 x 7.5 cm] on both bottom side corners on each side.

8. Pinch the bottom corners, to align the side seam on top of the centerline at the bottom.

9. Sew along the marked line, which will make the end parts look like a triangle.

10. Trim off ½" [12 mm] from the stitched line **(f)**.

11. Place the lining inside the exterior fabric with wrong sides facing.

12. Fold the top edges with ½" [12 mm] seam allowances facing next to each other, and pin/clip the two layers together. Make sure to match side seams neatly.

13. Using a fabric marker, mark points 5½" [14 cm] in from the side seams on both sides of the bag opening, for the handles **(g)**.

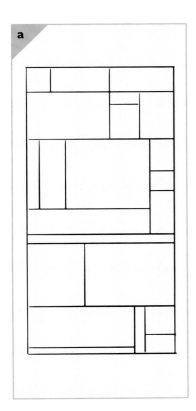

a

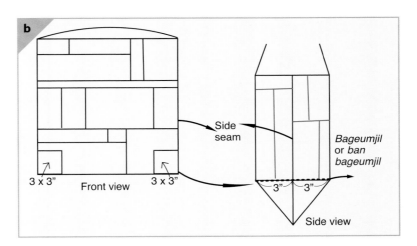

b

Side seam

Bageumjil or ban bageumjil

3 x 3"   Front view   3 x 3"

3"   3"

Side view

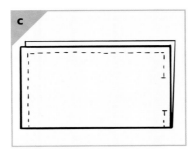

c

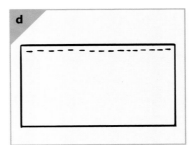

d

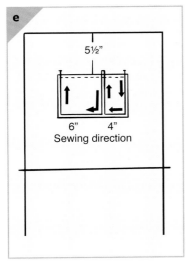

e

5½"

6"   4"
Sewing direction

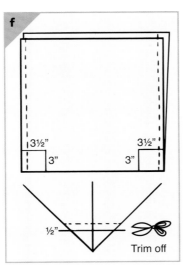

f

3½"   3½"

3"   3"

½"   Trim off

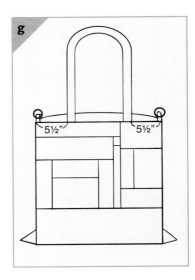

g

5½"   5½"

Tabs

1. Cut 2 pieces 3" [7.5 cm] square for side seam tabs.

2. Fold in half, right side out, with seam allowances tucked inside.

3. Stitch along the long side.

4. Mark 1" [2.5 cm] down from the top folded part with a fabric marker.

5. Place and pin tabs on each side seam, between the lining and outer fabric **(a)**.

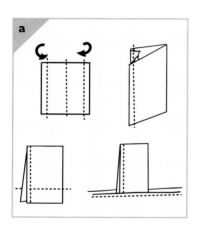

Leather handle option

1. Cut 4 pieces 3 x 4" [7.5 x 10 cm] for the leather strap tabs.

2. Fold in half, right side out, with seam allowances tucked inside. Stitch along the long side.

3. Mark 1½" [3.8 cm] from the top folded part with fabric marker.

4. Pin tabs at the marks you made for the handles in step 13 of 'Lining and pocket'.

5. Sew the exterior fabric and lining together around the top edge, including through the six pinned tabs.

6. ¼" [6 mm] below the stitch line, sew around the top of the tote one more time.

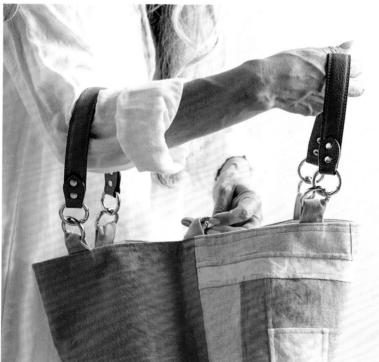

FINISHING

Fabric handle

1. Cut 2 pieces 2¼ x 24" [5.7 x 60 cm] of darker color fabric (A).

2. Cut 2 pieces 2¼ x 24" [5.7 x 60 cm] of lighter color fabric (B).

3. Fold a ½" [12 mm] seam allowance on each side. Place A and B together with wrong sides facing and seam allowances tucked inside. Stitch on both sides **(b)**.

4. Place handles on the marks you made in step 13 of 'Lining and pocket', with 1" [2.5 cm] seam allowance.

5. Sew exterior fabric and linings together around the top edge, including through the tabs and handles.

6. ¼" [6 mm] below the stitch line, sew around the top of the tote one more time.

7. Attach two trigger snap o-rings in the tabs.

8. Connect the two o-rings to make a trapezoid shaped tote.

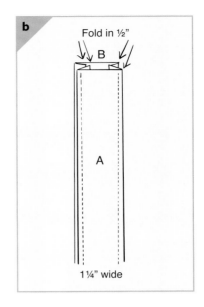

Leather handle

1. Attach six trigger snap o-rings in the tabs.

2. Attach leather handles **(c)**.

3. Connect the two o-rings on the sides to make a trapezoid shaped tote.

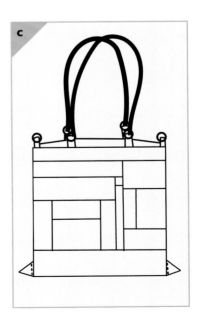

Ssamsol Jogakbo

This is another *jogakbo* where I used materials from my backyard dye studio. Some fabrics are dyed with natural dyes, and others with synthetic dyes. I like how these colors go well with each other. It was a fun process playing with colors and the orientation of shapes. This piece took me a while to finish, because it was buried in a pile of hand-dyed fabric, and I forgot about it. When I found a half-made *jogakbo*, it delighted me to remember that autumn day dyeing fabrics in my backyard.

FINISHED SIZE

Width: 24½" [62 cm]
Length: 25½" [65 cm]

These are the finished measurements of my piece, but you can make yours any size you wish. Please enjoy the process of free-form design.

MATERIALS

- 2–3 yards [1.8–2.7 m] ramie (various colors/sizes)
- Cotton thread
- Needle

Stitches used

Ssamsol (flat felled seam) – see p.52.

INSTRUCTIONS

Have fun constructing with slanted *ssamsol*!

Window Covering

I love the texture of linen. Freshly laundered linen bedding gives such comfort. This *jogakbo* window covering was created using some of my worn-out bed linen. It filters direct sunlight during the day, but my room still gets the warmth of the sun and plenty of light. Wherever you live, linen is likely to be an easier material to find than ramie. I recommend you try working with different weights of linen before you start a big project.

For this *jogakbo*, I wanted to create rectilinear shapes, and played with different sizes of rectangles in the composition. Sometimes it is very enjoyable to work with one set idea in mind.

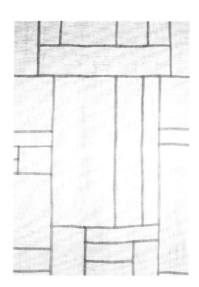

FINISHED SIZE

Measure your own window and create a piece to fit.

MATERIALS

- Linen or ramie, or your choice of fabric. However, I don't recommend using silk fabric for a window covering, as sunlight will damage silk and the fabric will fade.
- Cotton thread
- Needle

Stitches used

Ssamsol (flat felled seam) – see p.52.

INSTRUCTIONS

1. Use *ssamsol* to build your block until the piece is big enough to cover your window **(a)**.

2. Once your piece is large enough, add a solid (not pieced) 3½" [9 cm] x [width of your work] piece of fabric on top of your work **(b)**.

3. Fold at the seam to the back of the *jogakbo* and finish with a double-fold hem (see p.53). I used a ½" [12 mm] seam allowance for the double-fold hem **(c)**.

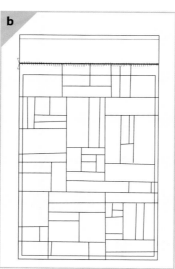

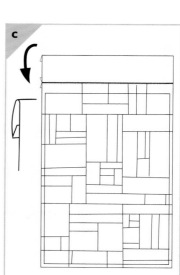

Barbara's Boat Coaster

One day, my friend Barbara sent me a photo of a coaster that she saw while traveling and said, 'You might be able to figure out how this was made!' This piqued my curiosity, and I started to fold and unfold square pieces of fabric to find the secret behind this design. Finally, my 'aha' moment arrived! I worked out how Barbara's boat coaster was made and now I can share it with you. The original coaster was made with two solid square fabrics, and I decided to add some *jogakbo* details.

FINISHED SIZE

5½" [14 cm] square before folded into a boat shape

MATERIALS

- 6" [15 cm] patchwork squares x 2
  You will need:
  Scraps of fabric of your choice to make a *jogakbo*-style square block.
  I used my *jogakbo* printed cotton, *chunpo* (ramie and silk blend fabric) and naturally dyed linen
- Cotton thread
- Needle

Stitches used
Gamchimjil (whip stitch) – see p.44.
Homjil (running stitch) – see p.43.

Notes
This project uses a ¼" [6 mm] seam allowance throughout.

INSTRUCTIONS

1. Sew small scraps together from the right side of the fabric. Make two *jogakbo* pieces, 6" [15 cm] square **(a)**.

2. Mark by scoring a ¼" [6 mm] seam allowance and fold from the right side toward the wrong side of the fabric.

3. Place two pieces together and pin around four edges. Sew and connect two pieces together **(b)**.

4. Score a diagonal line in the middle. Once you score a line, fold one small triangle from the top, and fold another from the bottom toward the scored middle line **(c)**.

5. Gently pull out the top and the bottom middle lines with both hands until a boat shape forms **(d)**.

6. Secure the tip of both triangles on the bottom of the boat using a small stitch **(e)**.

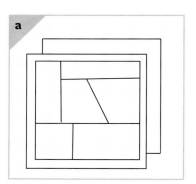

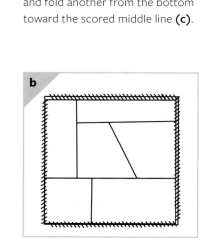

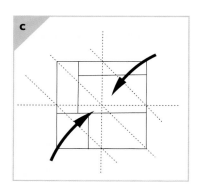

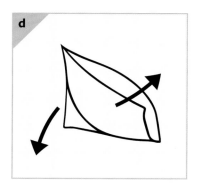

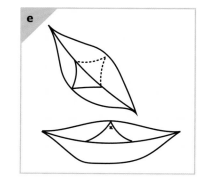

Book Sleeve

Organizing my daily schedule is an important task for me, and I use not only my computer and phone, but also my old-school planner. I made a well-fitting jacket for my planner and use it every day. If you like to keep a journal, you can make this cover to protect precious moments and memories.

FINISHED SIZE
Measure your book or planner, and make it to fit.

MATERIALS
- *Sukgosa* (Korean silk gauze)
- Silk thread
- Needle

Stitches used
Homjil (running stitch) – see p.43.
Gamchimjil (whip stitch) – see p.44.
Gonggeureugi (blind stitch) – see p.47.
Settam sangchim (decorative triple stitch) – see p.46.

Notes
This project uses a ¼" [6 mm] seam allowance throughout.

INSTRUCTIONS

1. Measure the planner or notebook you want to cover. These will be the measurements for the exterior of the book sleeve **(a)**.

2. Using scraps of fabrics, make a *jogakbo* block to your book measurements, using *gamchimjil*.

3. Place right sides of the *jogakbo* block and the solid fabric together.

4. Sew with *homjil* around all four sides, leaving a small opening **(b)**.

5. Using the opening, turn inside out. Sew the opening shut with *gonggeureugi*.

6. If you want to add *settam sangchim*, stitch them on the right side **(c)**.

7. Fold the two sides inward to make pockets and pin them to secure. Sew the top and bottom of the folds with *gamchimjil* **(d)**.

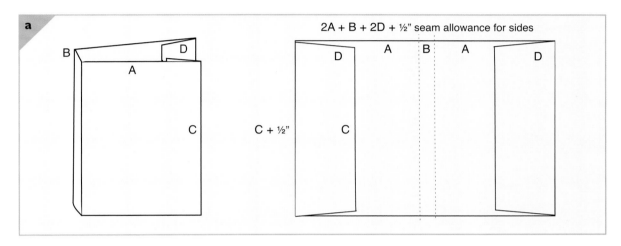

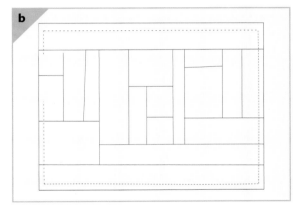

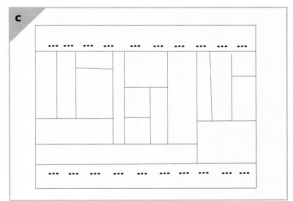

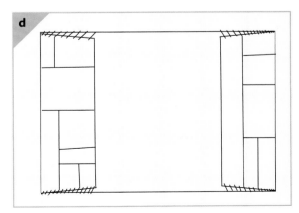

Yeouijumun Brooch

I love sewing, making and wearing what I create. I first started using this color combination for my piece 'Luminous I' (see p.144), and gradually sized down to *jumeoni* and brooches. Making tiny *yeouijumun* can be a bit challenging if you are making this pattern for the first time. You can start with bigger pieces of square fabric to practice, and eventually work smaller, just like I did when I started making mine.

FINISHED SIZE

Width: 2¼" [5.7 cm]
Length: 2¼" [5.7 cm]

MATERIALS

- *Sukgosa* (Korean silk gauze). You can use lightweight cotton voile instead of *sukgosa* if you prefer.
  You will need:
  2½" [6.4 cm] squares x 4
  ½" [12 mm] square for *yeouijumun* inserts x 4
  2¾ x 5" [7 x 12.5 cm] for the back layer x 1
  2" [5 cm] for *bakjwi maedeup* or beads/pearls to decorate points x 4
- Cotton/silk thread
- Needle
- Magnet button

Stitches used

Gamchimjil (whip stitch) – see p.44.
Homjil (running stitch) – see p.43.
Ban bageumjil (half back stitch) – see p.46.

INSTRUCTIONS

1. Cut a 2½" [6.4 cm] square piece of fabric and score ¼" [6 mm] seam allowance lines around four corners. Fold and iron the creased lines.

2. Mark the center point by creasing and folding diagonally and horizontally.

3. Thread a needle with a single thread and make a knot at the end.

4. Put the needle through the center mark from the back of the fabric **(a)**.

5. Go through the four corners and pull the needle and thread to the center **(b** and **c)**.

6. Put the needle through the center point to move the needle and thread to the bottom. Iron the folded lines **(d)**.

7. Turn upside-down and put the needle through the 4 corners again **(e)**.

8. Put the needle through the bottom and tie a knot. Now the square is 1" [2.5 cm] **(f)**.

9. Make three more units using steps 1–8 **(g)**.

10. Connect two units using *gamchimjil* **(h)**.

11. Repeat until you have four connected units **(i)**.

12. Cut a ½" [12 mm] square of contrasting color fabric. Trim off all four sides to get a curved line. This will help you manage the next step of folding and stitching edges. Trimming off the sides will make the finished line less bulky when you fold edges over **(j)**.

13. Place the fabric in the middle of the stitched units and baste it.

14. Gently fold the four surrounding bias edges toward the center square.

15. Stitch on the folded edges using *homjil* or *ban bageumjil*. Five to six stitches on each side would be ideal. Now you have a finished four-piece *yeouijumun* block **(k)**.

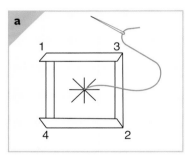

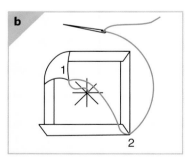

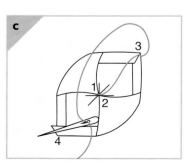

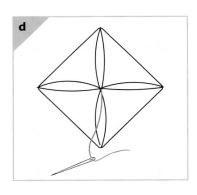

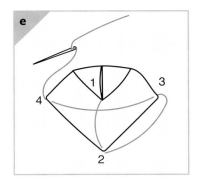

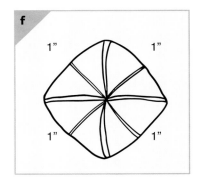

1"   1"

1"   1"

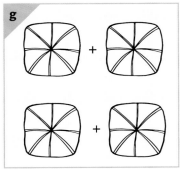

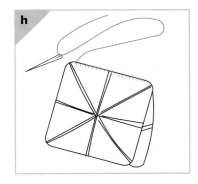

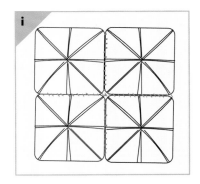

For the base:

1. Prepare 2¾ x 5" [7 x 12.5 cm] piece of fabric and mark ¼" [6 mm] seam allowance lines around four corners.

2. Fold in half lengthwise, from the right side to the wrong side of the fabric **(l)**.

3. Fold and tuck seam allowances and connect three sides with *gamchimjil* **(m)**.

4. Place a *yeouijumun* block on top of the base and secure with pins. Add pearls or beads on the corner to decorate the surface and to secure two parts (the base and the block) together.

5. Sew or glue one half of a magnet button on the back, and use the other half to fix your *yeouijumun* brooch to your clothing.

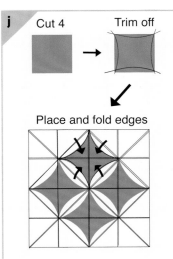

Cut 4   Trim off

Place and fold edges

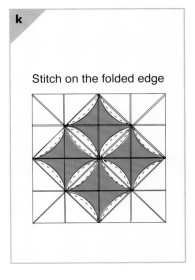

Stitch on the folded edge

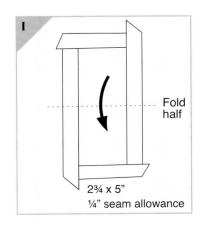

Fold half

2¾ x 5"
¼" seam allowance

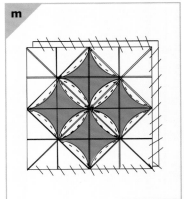

A Good Luck Charm (*Goebul Norigae*)

Goebul norigae, a small triangular shape decorated with colorful thread, is considered a good luck charm as the three points can cast out or ward off misfortune or evil spirits. Mothers make these and have their children wear them for protection. *Norigae* is a traditional Korean accessory for women that is tied on the waistband of a *chima* (skirt) or *goreum* (a single bowed sash of a *jeogori*, a short jacket). I made a few of these so I can wear them as an accessory or attach to my purse, to keep myself happy and lucky.

FINISHED SIZE

3½ x 14" [9 x 36 cm]
3½ x 13" [9 x 33 cm]
3½ x 6½" [9 x 16.5 cm]

MATERIALS

- Plain woven silk or cotton
  You will need:
  3" [7.5 cm] square to make a triangle (for a smaller triangle, use a piece 2½" [6.4 cm] square)
  1½ x 30" [3.8 x 75 cm] piece (for the long strap)
  1½ x 12" [3.8 x 30 cm] pieces x 2 (for different colored strips)
- Sewing thread
- Thread to make tassels
- *Satteugi* (heavier-weight silk thread)
- Needle
- Stuffing

Stitches used
Gamchimjil (whip stitch) – see p.44.
Satteugi (cross stitch) – see p.48.

INSTRUCTIONS

1. Mark a ¼" [6 mm] seam allowance around the square **(a)**.

2. Fold from the right side of the fabric toward the wrong side **(b)**.

3. Score a diagonal line and fold the square into a triangle.

4. Tuck folded seam allowances to get a neatly folded corner. Repeat on the other side **(c)**.

5. *Gamchimjil* on one side of the triangle. Repeat on the other side but leave 1" [2.5 cm] to fill inside with stuffing **(d)**.

6. *Satteugi* on the previous *gamchimjil* stitched line to cover stitches and decorate. Now you are done making a *goebul* **(e)**.

7. Make a tassel (see p.70) using colorful threads and attach to both bottom corners of the triangle.

8. Fold the fabric for the strap in half.

9. Place the *goebul* between the folded strap and secure with small star-shaped stitches above and below. If you wish, you can make multiple triangles, placing star-shaped stitches between each triangle **(f**, **g** and **h)**.

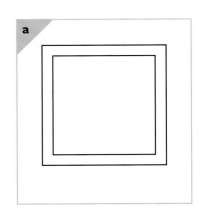

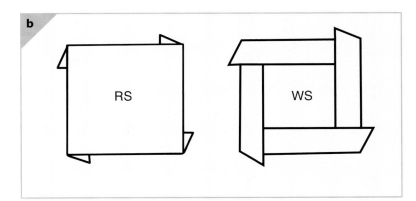

RS

WS

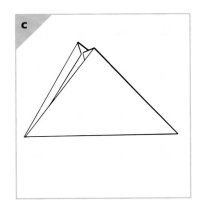

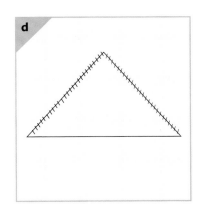

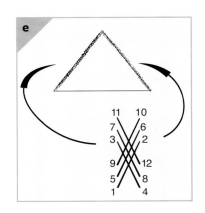

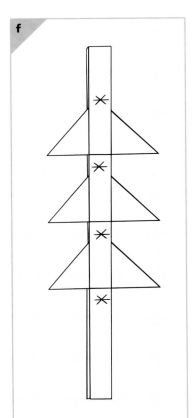

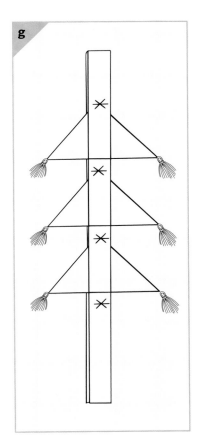

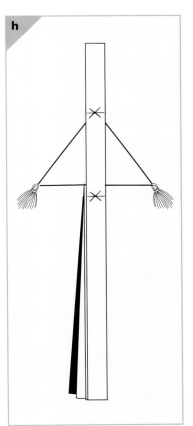

Wind Chime
(Punggyeong)

When I think about Buddhist temples in Korea, the first things that I visualize are the wind chimes at the eaves of the shrine. They usually have a bell and a wooden fish shape. The bells sound when the wind blows, and the blue sky and fish remind me of the sea. This *jogakbo*-style patchwork wind chime was born from these memories. My wind chime makes me picture a vessel, floating upside-down in the blue sky.

FINISHED SIZE

Height: 4 x 4½" [10 x 11.4 cm] not including cord and bell

MATERIALS

- Remnants of fabrics to make a 9 x 10" [23 x 25 cm] patchwork block
- Sewing thread
- 1 yard [90 cm] cord
- 1–2 beads
- 1 brass bell
- 9 x 10" [23 x 25 cm] template to measure patchwork piece (½" [12 mm] seam allowance included) – see pp.154–155.
- Needle

Stitches used

Gamchimjil (whip stitch) – see p.44.

INSTRUCTIONS

1. Stitch small pieces of fabric together using *gamchimjil* until you have a 9 x 10" [23 x 25 cm] patchwork block **(a)**.

2. Fold a ½" [12 mm] seam allowance along both 9" [23 cm] sides. Place these sides together and *gamchimjil* to make a cylinder **(b** and **c)**.

3. Take one end of the cylinder and fold it down to make another cylinder, 4½" [11.4 cm] in diameter and 4" [10 cm] long.

4. Connect the open ends using *gamchimjil*.

5. Fold the top part to make a 'plus' shape **(d)**.

6. Stitch through at the top to hold the shape **(e)**.

7. Fold 1 yard [90 cm] cord in half and make *dorae maedeup* (double crossed knot, see p.57) or add a bead 4–5" [10–12.5 cm] from the top.

8. Make a *yeonbong maedeup* (lotus bud knot, see p.58) and *dorae maedeup* (or you can use a bead or two instead of *dorae maedeup*).

9. Attach the cord in the center of the wind chime and attach a bell at the bottom **(f)**.

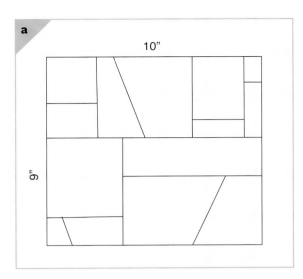

a

10"

9"

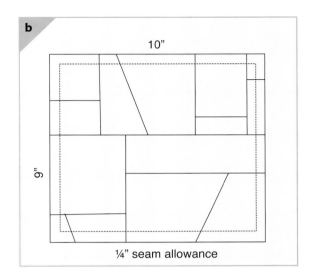

b

10"

9"

¼" seam allowance

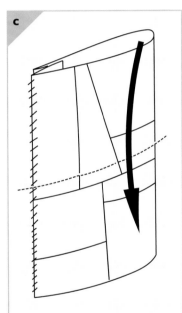

c

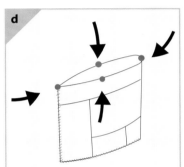

d

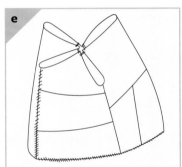

e

f

Dumpling-Shaped Square Mobile
(Mandu)

When I introduced this mobile during my workshop, one of my students said that the shape reminded them of *mandu* (a dumpling commonly eaten at *Seollal*) – and not only the shape, but the making process, too. Start with a flat dumpling wrapper, stuff it with yummy ingredients, and seal to make a shape. This fabric *mandu* can be stuffed with good wishes and happy thoughts. I sometimes stuff these with scraps from my sewing, such as leftover short threads or tiny fabric selvages.

Sheer fabrics such as *oksa* (sheer, stiff silk), organza, and *mosi* (ramie) are wonderful materials to make this mobile. Using very simple shapes and stitch techniques, you can make decorations for yourself or to share with others.

Using *gamchimjil*, you will be able to make these precise 3D shapes. This can be a great idea for whimsical mobiles, garlands, or wearable accessories. If you are comfortable making *mandu* with a 4" [10 cm] square, try increasing or decreasing the size. I love to save 1" [2.5 cm] square scraps to make tiny earrings and smaller-scale mobiles.

MATERIALS

- *Oksa* (sheer and stiff silk), organza, or *mosi* (ramie) – 4" [10 cm] square makes one *mandu*
- Thread/cord for hanging
- Cotton thread
- Needle

Stitches used
Gamchimjil (whip stitch) – see p.44.

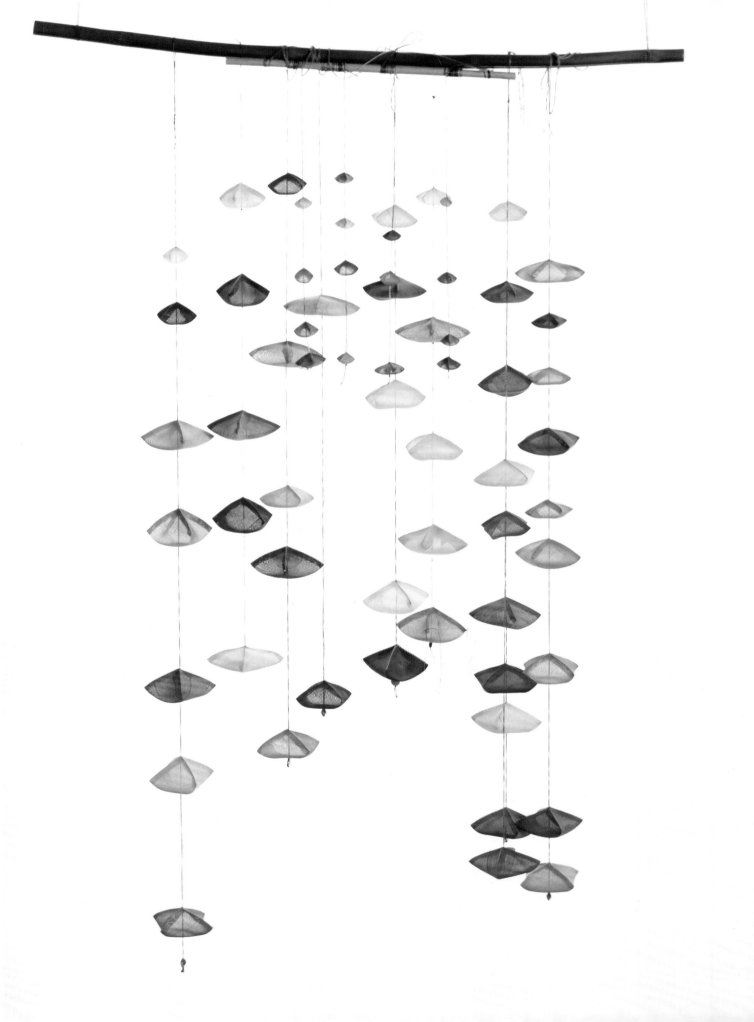

INSTRUCTIONS

1. Cut square fabric (any size is fine) with a ¼" [6 mm] seam allowance on all four sides **(a)**.

2. Fold seam allowances from the outside to the inside of the fabric **(b)**.

3. Fold the square in half **(c)**.

4. Stitch from A to B, then from C to D using *gamchimjil* **(d)**.

5. Fold the opening part in half and pinch E and F to place A and C together.

6. Stitch from E to F using *gamchimjil* **(e)**.

7. Make multiple *mandu*. Using a piece of knotted thread, string them together to make a mobile, adding as many *mandu* to each length of string as you wish **(f)**.

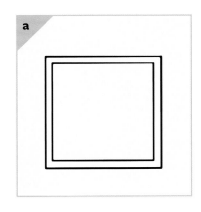

a

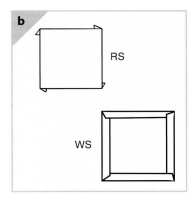

b

RS

WS

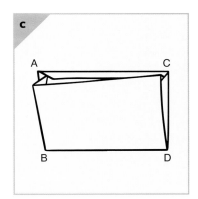

c

A   C

B   D

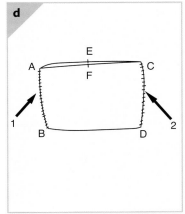

d

A   E   C
           F

B   D

1   2

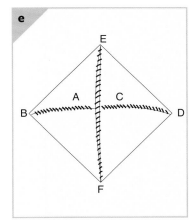

e

E

B   A   C   D

F

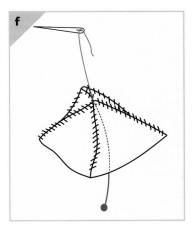

f

Gwijumeoni Sachet

Since traditional Korean clothes don't have pockets, Korean people carried *jumeoni* to hold their personal belongings. *Jumeoni* are drawstring pouches made from fabric, paper, or leather. There are many kinds of pouches of different shapes, made with varying materials, and with multiple uses. *Durujumeoni* is round, *gwijumeoni* has an angular shape resembling ears, and *yakjumeoni* is used to carry or store medicine. I made these *gwijumeoni* to hold *bok* (happiness) and dried lavender from my garden.

FINISHED SIZE

Width: 4½" [11.4 cm]
Height: 3¾" [9.5 cm]

MATERIALS

- 5 x 6" [12.5 x 15 cm] fabric piece for the exterior of the pouch. A sheer fabric is lovely when it complements the lining fabric color (Fabric A)
- 5 x 10" [12.5 x 25 cm] fabric piece for the lining. This fabric should be tightly woven to keep the sachet contents secure (Fabric B)
- 24" [60 cm] strands of string or thread x 3. I used sashiko thread dyed with indigo and persimmon, but you can choose any ⅙–⅛" [2–3 mm] cord
- Awl
- Hook or tapestry needle for threading cord

Stitches used

Bageumjil (back stitch) – see p.45.
Ban bageumjil (half back stitch) – see p.46.
Gamchimjil (whip stitch) – see p.44.

Notes

This project uses a seam allowance of ¼" [6 mm] throughout.

INSTRUCTIONS

1. With right sides together, pin the 5" [12.5 cm] edges of the fabric pieces to each other **(a)**.

2. Sew together using *ban bageumjil* or *bageumjil* **(b** and **c)**.

3. Press seam toward fabric A **(d)**.

4. Fold to line up seams and pin together. * and ** should meet together **(e)**.

5. Mark 2" [5 cm] in from the center fold of fabric A. Sew from the fold of fabric A to the 2" [5 cm] mark **(f)**.

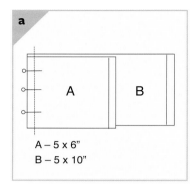

A – 5 x 6"
B – 5 x 10"

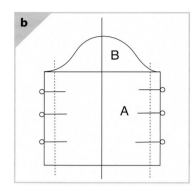

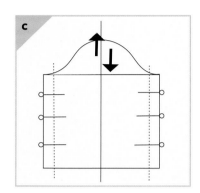

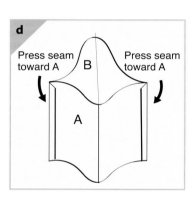

Press seam toward A   Press seam toward A

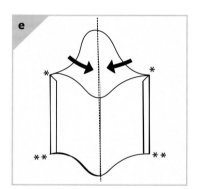

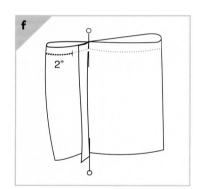

2"

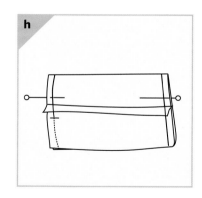

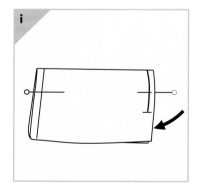

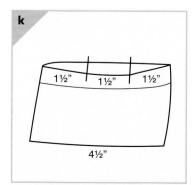

1½"   1½"   1½"

4½"

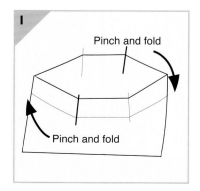

Pinch and fold

Pinch and fold

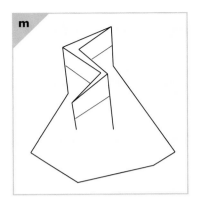

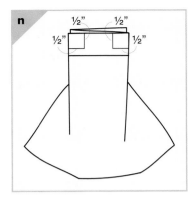

6. Fold the piece in half, lining up center folds of fabric A and fabric B **(g)**.

7. Sew through all layers from the 2" [5 cm] mark to the center fold of fabric B **(h)**.

8. Sew through all layers on the other edge, from center fold of fabric A to the center fold of fabric B.

9. Using the opening on one side, turn your piece inside out. Fold seam allowance inside **(i)**.

10. *Gamchimjil* the opening closed **(j)**.

11. Turn your piece inside out one more time (now you can't see any stitches from the outside). With fabric A at the top, mark 1½" [3.8 cm] in from the sides. You should have three 1½" [3.8 cm] sections **(k)**.

12. Pinch or press each of these marks from the outside. Your piece should be gently hexagonal.

13. Fold the front-left and back-right pinches. Hold the top of your piece together between the front-left and back-right pinches **(l)**.

14. Accordion fold the top of your piece, folding both pieces down clockwise **(m)**.

15. Clip or pin the top of your pouch together and flat.

16. Mark two dots for string – I marked ½" [12 mm] from the top and sides **(n)**.

17. Carefully make holes with an awl **(o)**.

18. Braid three strands into a tricolor cord. Using a loop turner, hook, or large tapestry needle, pull your cord through both holes. Tie a bow and you've made a *gwijumeoni* **(p)**!

9
My Work
and Collection

Works

1. Hope I

In 2020, during the pandemic, I was busy making face masks for my family, my neighbors, and essential workers. A friend of mine sent me boxes of muslin she wasn't using anymore. I made and shared lots of masks and started to make *jogakbo* using the leftover fabric from mask making. As these pieces grew, I felt that the hope for a better future was also growing in my mind.

Materials: Cotton muslin, cotton thread
Technique: *Ssamsol* with sewing machine
Dimensions: 118 x 42" [300 x 107 cm] each

2. Remnants of Memory

When I found handwoven indigo-dyed cotton at an antique store in Korea, I began to imagine the memories of conversations that cloth has carried over time. This train of thought sparked my creativity, and I began piecing together small fragments of fabric, adding more and more as I worked. Sometimes, I planned my next moves, but other times it grew as if it had its own intention. I just enjoyed the rhythm of stitching, the result beyond my control. I appreciate the beauty that results from the long, slow process of hand stitching – a meditative act that creates an unexpected, spontaneous result.

Materials: Vintage handwoven cotton, ramie dyed in indigo, safflower, and fiber-reactive dye
Technique: *Ssamsol* and *homjil*
Dimensions: 63½ x 61" [161 x 155 cm]

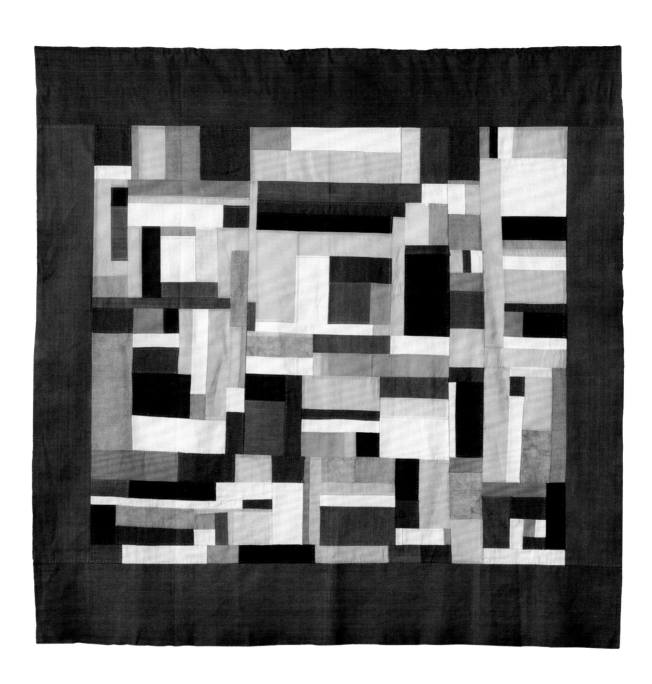

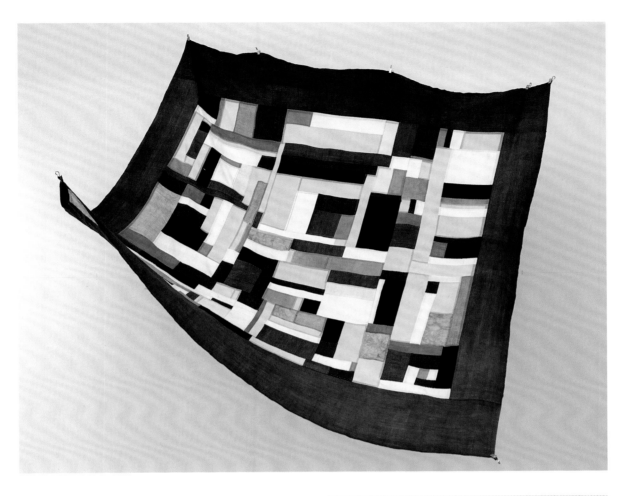

3. Westerlies

One day, I got a package from a friend in Tokyo. She had sent me naturally dyed ramie and silk, a process she had learned from a teacher in Korea. Her kind heart and friendship traveled across the Pacific Ocean in the form of dyed fabrics, with the help of westerly winds. Despite distance and conflicts between countries and cultures, kindness can have a positive impact across the world.

Materials: *Oksa* and *mosi* (ramie) dyed in indigo, onion, loquat, and mallow leaves
Technique: *Ssamsol*
Dimensions: 39 x 43" [99 x 109 cm]

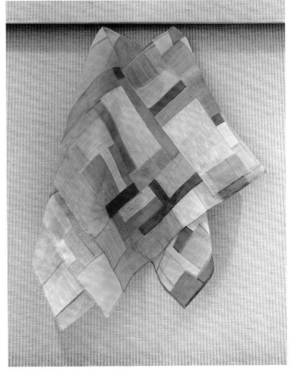

4. Dreamy Blue

I love to dye fabrics in my backyard, and indigo is one of my favorite dyes. The San Francisco Bay area, where I live, has a rich fiber art and textile culture, and resources are easy to find. I was fortunate to have opportunities to learn about natural dyeing, including indigo dyeing, from wonderful teachers. I was able to expand my horizons by taking workshops, meeting artists, and sharing common interests.

I tried for three years to cultivate indigo from seed that I got from fellow artists. The first year, I was excited and impatient to get started; I didn't know that I needed to start seeds indoors to transplant later. In the second year, I was able to get seedlings and transplant them to my backyard, but bugs ate most of them within a week. Finally, in the third year, I was able to grow indigo and enjoyed using it for fresh indigo dye during the summer. My trial-and-error indigo growing taught me to be patient, humble, accepting, and to embrace my limits.

I dyed *hanji bidan* (silk and mulberry paper blend fabric) with indigo and created this work. I sewed pieces with red silk thread, and this represents my eager yet impatient attempts to master indigo growing by myself.

Materials: *Hanji bidan*
Technique: *Ssamsol*
Dimensions: 34 x 37" [86 x 94 cm]

5. Going Home

My friend Carlene in Hawaii encouraged me to learn the fabric-dyeing process and gave me a week-long intensive dye lesson in her home studio. I used fabrics that I dyed with her to create this project. This piece always reminds me of Hawaii's blue ocean and sandy beaches.

Materials: Ramie
Technique: *Ssamsol*
Dimensions: 21 x 44" [53 x 112 cm]

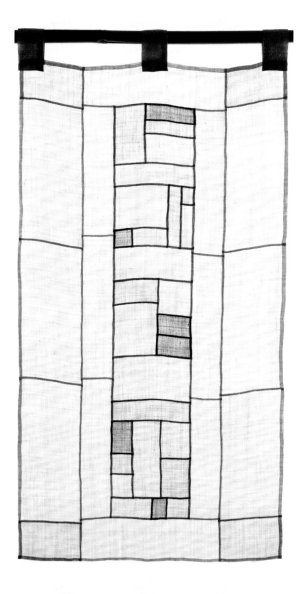

6. My Cup of Tea

I learned from Ana Lisa that easy and effective dye materials can be found in your cupboard. She taught me how to dye silk with tea. Tannin-rich tea and coffee can easily bind to fabrics without using mordants.

I was thrilled to use my favorite drinks as my dye bath for organza and cotton. During the fabric-dyeing process, the aroma and rich color infused and saturated the fabric.

Materials: Tea- and coffee-dyed organza, cotton
Technique: *Ssamsol*
Dimensions: 24 x 63" [60 x 160 cm]

7. Winter

In the winter of 2011, I spent some time helping my family in Korea. Even though I grew up in Korea, two decades of living in California made me forget how cold it gets there. The coldness and sadness of winter made me feel numb for a while. As I hadn't planned to stay long, I left my seven sewing friends behind.

However, a desire to sew and stitch something made me persevere even with limited resources. All I had was a pair of scissors, a needle and plain white cotton thread for basting bed sheets. I went to the fabric market and bought a bolt of black ramie and started this *jogakbo*. I used fabric scissors instead of a rotary cutter, my fingernails instead of a bone folder. While I went through this sad and difficult time, the simple act of making supported me and helped me to move on.

Materials: Ramie, cotton thread
Technique: *Gamchimjil*
Dimensions: 35 x 36" [89 x 91 cm]

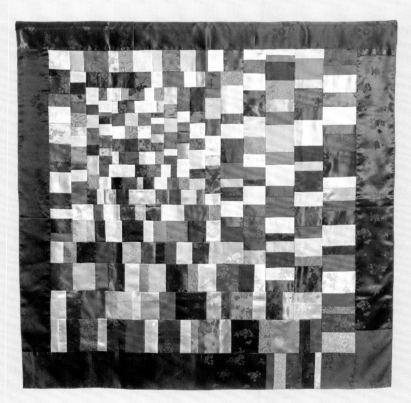

8. Bidan Kkum

Bidan is one of the names for silk fabrics, and I always like how this word sounds. It reminds me of the smooth, soft, warm, elegant, shiny silk surface. I used lots of pieces of old and new colorful *bidan jogak* including my mother's old *chima* (skirt) and *jeogori* (jacket) to make this work. After I added the border and back layer, I felt that this piece would comfort me just as I was comforted sleeping in my childhood house, feeling the soft voice of my grandmother. *Kkum* means 'dream' in Korean.

Materials: *Bidan* (Korean silk satin and brocade)
Technique: *Gamchimjil*
Dimensions: 58½ x 59½" [149 x 151 cm]

9. After Rain

Natural dye practice in my backyard was one of the creative activities I most enjoyed during the pandemic of 2020 and 2021. This gave me a chance to slow down, to look around at my surroundings, and to learn patience until I got the result I was looking for. This process cleared my mind... and my stash of remnants! When I made this piece, I mostly used materials I dyed myself in my backyard and leftover fabrics from previous projects.

Materials: Ramie, linen, cotton, organza
Technique: *Ssamsol*
Dimensions: 35 x 38" [89 x 97 cm]

I have made these works as an homage to the enormous labor and care of the Joseon Dynasty mother-of-pearl artisans who prepared and inlaid the natural materials on wooden surfaces. Although the materials are different, I patched the small pieces of fabric together to transmit the essence and philosophy embedded in Joseon *najeon chilgi* (mother-of-pearl lacquerware). These are my interpretations of my traditions, as well as a reinterpretation of my native culture.

Materials: *Sukgosa* (Korean silk gauze), *yangdan* (silk satin and brocade), *nobang* (organza)
Technique: *Yeouijumun, ssamsol*
Dimensions: 22" [56 cm] square

10. Luminous I, II

After I saw an exhibit at the Asian Art Museum in San Francisco, I was inspired by the luminous mother-of-pearl lacquerware. I used *yeouijumun* (jewel pattern) and *ssamsol* techniques to reproduce the feeling and process of Korean lacquerware onto fabric. The iridescent colors of mother-of-pearl on lacquerware reflect hidden efforts over time.

11. Luminous III, IV, V

After I created 'Luminous I', my mind was still wandering, and I had lots more to express and to experiment with, so I started my Luminous series. I used painting, layering, and stitching on the surface of fabric to create a mother-of-pearl effect.

Materials: *Nobang* (organza), *oksa*
Technique: *Ssamsol, gamchimjil, homjil, sangchim*
Dimensions: Luminous III 18½" [47 cm] square
Luminous IV 21 x 21½" [53 x 55 cm]
Luminous V 22 x 23½" [56 x 60 cm]

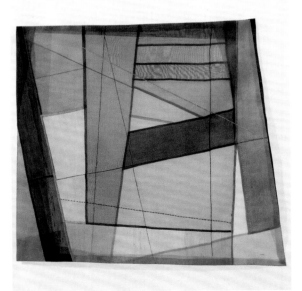

12. Strokes and Stitches

One year, when I came back home from Korea, I brought my father's calligraphy practice sheets with me. For over 50 years, he has practiced his calligraphy every morning. He is not a professional calligrapher, but he always wants to improve his strokes.

I have made this work as an homage to the enormous labor and care my father practiced daily on paper. I thought maybe this act, his way of meditation, can be part of my bojagi making process. I wanted to keep and remember his time and effort in my work so I can pay my respects to him. The lightweight paper he uses for his practice is called *hwa seon ji*. Since it is for practicing calligraphy, this paper is thinner and more fragile than *hanji* (Korean mulberry paper) and my father didn't care much about saving them. I made a big *yeouijumun* base and inserted my father's writing as jewel parts to transmit the essence and philosophy of his work.

This is my family collaboration piece, and I hope I can share my father's perseverance and diligence.

Materials: *Hwa seon ji*, cotton, cotton thread
Technique: *Yeouijumun*
Dimensions: 38 x 77" [97 x 196 cm]

13. Kkekki Jacket (Hovea pattern)

In 2021, I collaborated with Megan Nielsen Sewing Patterns on this Hovea jacket (named after a beautiful plant native to Western Australia). She was inspired by her three children's *Taekwondo dobok* (uniform) to create this simple yet stylish jacket. Megan asked me to create a jacket using my *jogakbo* as inspiration, giving me a chance to explore creating with different techniques, materials and styles. I used the *gopsol* (*kkekki*) technique to make this work. Each seam is made with three lines of fine stitching, and the finished seam is thin yet sturdy. Transparent organza is a perfect material for showcasing the *kkekki* technique.

Materials: *Nobang* (silk organza)
Technique: *Gopsol* (*kkekki*)
Dimensions: 62 x 35" [157 x 89 cm]

14. Abundance of Happiness

One autumn afternoon in 2018, I had a chance to visit the oQamoQa studio in Seoul, South Korea. I visited the studio with my friend Eunju, and we all had a magical time while we talked about creativity and how the act of tearing and gluing paper soothes the soul. One year later, I visited her studio again with my Korea Textile Tour group. We all sat around a big table, wearing very colorful aprons, and started tearing colorful papers. Sungok, the founder of oQamoQa, told us to feel free to tear, arrange, and glue to make whatever our hearts desired. Everybody in the room had such a joyful time! We talked and laughed like children. We all left the studio with our own colorful work, and Sungok created unique fabric patterns based on each person's creation.

oQamoQa's unique patterns are printed on fabrics, and they turn into thoughtfully designed products such as tote bags, sitting cushions, skirts, dresses, and robes. Their colors are whimsical, and I could definitely feel the positive energy from them.

When Sungok asked about a collaboration project in 2020, I thought about how her way of seeking happiness and mine are not too different. This is how this 'Double Happiness Project' was born. Six artists in five countries participated in this project, creating their own version of bojagi artworks. We had an exhibit at Bukchon Hanokcheong in Seoul, South Korea, in June 2021. 'Abundance of Happiness' was one of the works that I created for this project.

Instagram: @oqamoqa

Materials: oQamoQa's cotton remnants, *oksa*, *nobang*
Technique: *Ssamsol*
Dimensions: 31 x 35" [79 x 89 cm]

Memories in cloth – my bojagi collection

As I have more opportunities to travel and meet artists and artisans, my fascination with the concepts of bojagi, memory and time has grown. I began to collect old pieces, and these are a few in my collection.

Sambe (hemp) jogakbo

I met this *jogakbo* (**a**) in Kyoto, Japan, years ago. I went to the flea market to see old textiles, and one of the vendors was selling vintage textile items including this *sambe jogakbo*. It was folded, crinkled, and stained, but I saw the beauty of the time and memories held within it. It is hand-sewn using the *ssamsol* technique, but the maker's *gamchimjil* was a slightly different style to my usual one. I think this is quite an interesting piece to study in terms of sewing style.

Jogakbo

This *jogakbo* (**b**) obviously shows the time that it has endured. The silk and cotton fabric don't look the same as modern fabric I see in stores nowadays, and the tattered back layer is a sign of use. Because of the damage, this piece was able to come to me instead of to an antique store or another collector.

The *jogakbo* (**c**) shows signs of fabric recycling and improvisational construction on both the front and back.

Subo

I have three *subo* in my collection, and each of them are quite unique and interesting. These are all about 1 pok in size, with one or two straps.

I assume that these were used for wrapping and storing small objects.

The first *subo* was embroidered on a chrysanthemum-patterned brocade (**d**), and I see the maker's well-thought-out design works with the fabric pattern. The back of this *subo* is lined with flower-patterned silk featuring the character for 'longevity'. The word *bugi* was embroidered with flowers, and I suspect this is either a misspelling of *bugwi* (prosperity), or it might be an old way of spelling that word. If it was a mistake, then the maker might not have been very well educated, but the wishes for prosperity were well-imbued in this subo. If the spelling is old, that means this *subo* is older than I am. Isn't research fascinating?

The second and third ones are gifts from an artist in Andong. She didn't make these, but one of her family members did, a long time ago. The top layer was embroidered on silk fabric, and I see birds, tree branches, and flowers (**e**). These are all symbols of happiness, prosperity and fertility. The other *subo* shows embroidered fish and flower petals (**f**). The bright color blocks pieced together remind me of *saekdong*, while the black border frames the bright colors and design, bringing them into focus. These two *subo* are lined with *mumyeong* (plain woven cotton).

I appreciate the labor that went into making these bojagi, and the good intentions and joy their makers might have felt. I also want to celebrate the bojagi's previous utilitarian life, and its current second life as an admired and studied art form.

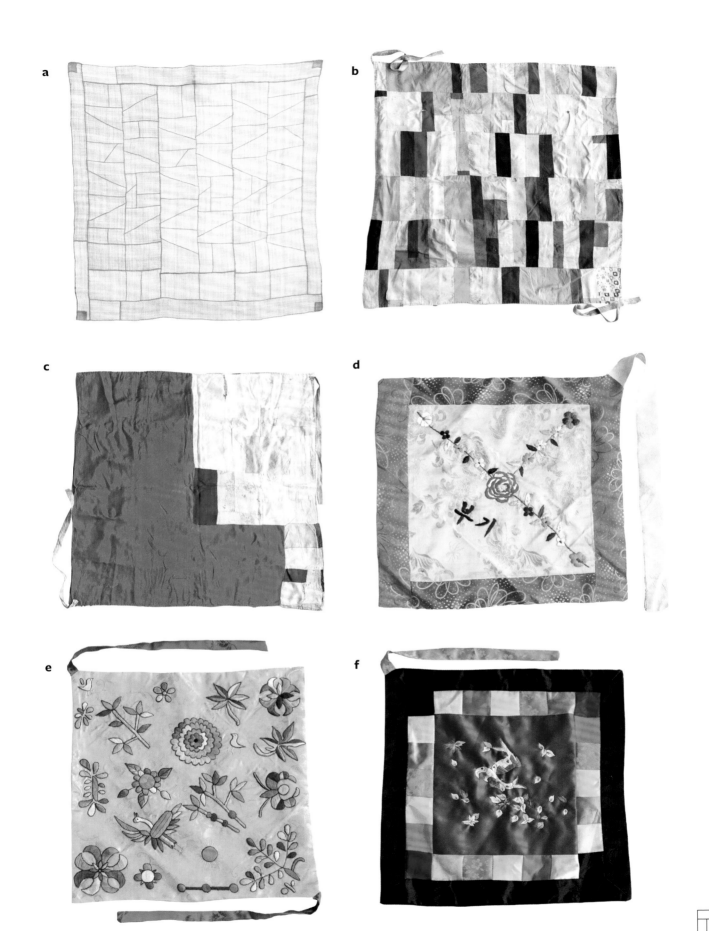

Templates

Lotus Leaf Mat 1
(p.72)

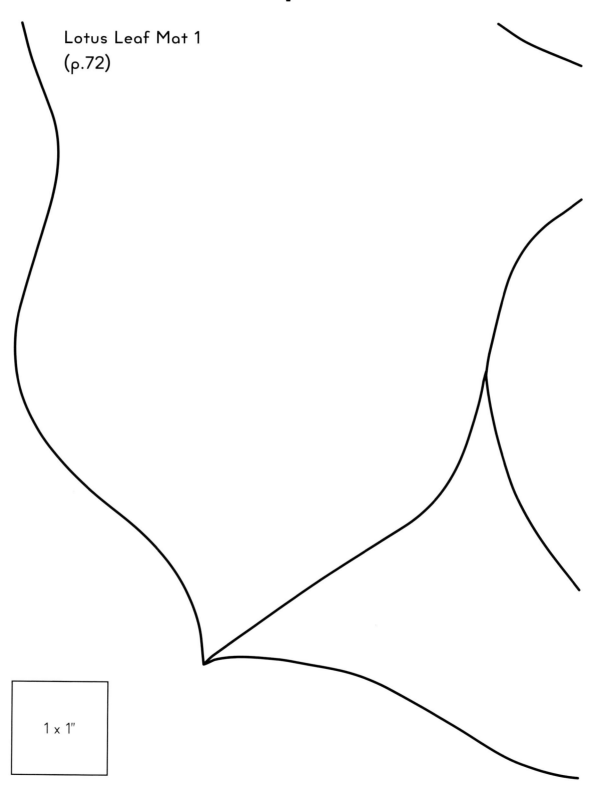

1 x 1"

Lotus Leaf Mat 2

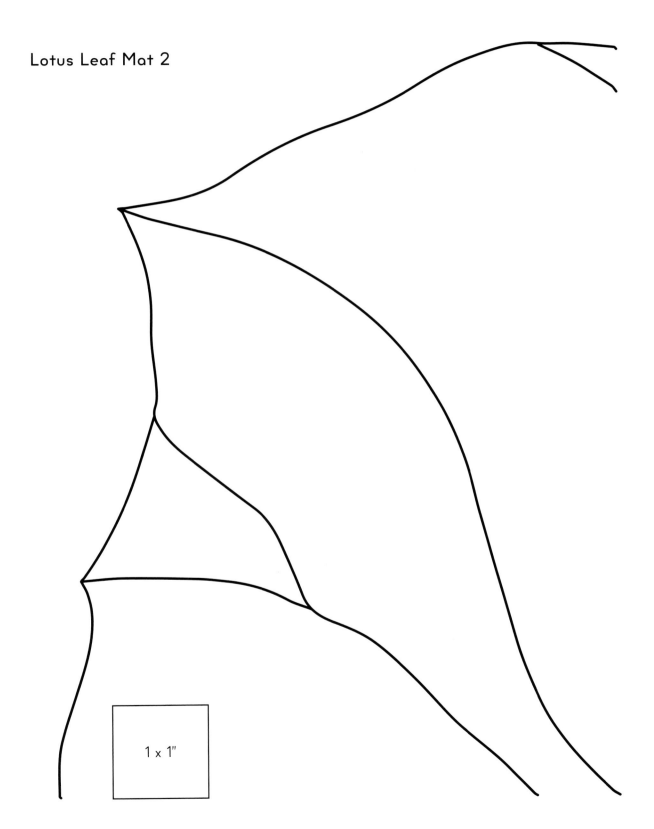

1 x 1"

Lotus Leaf Mat 3

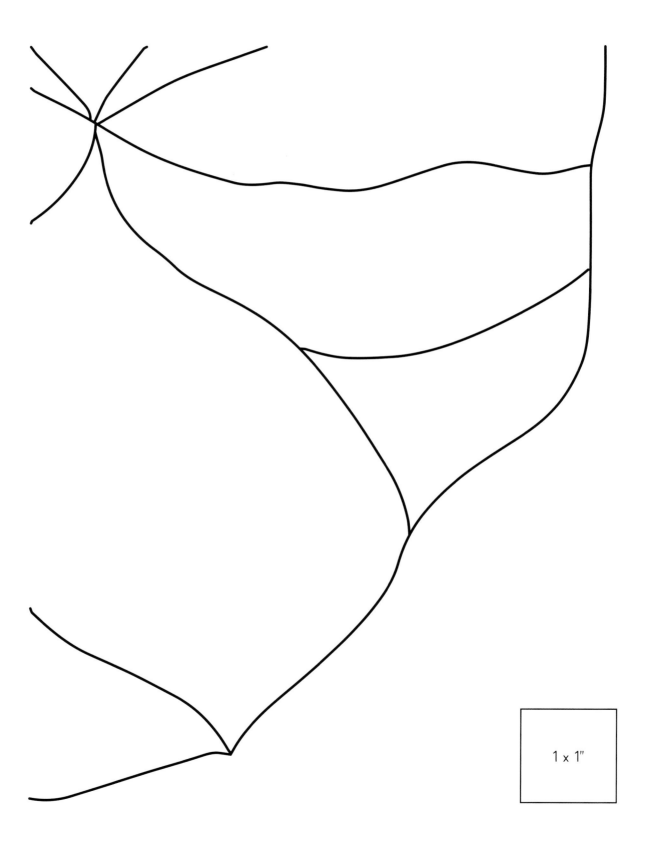

1 x 1"

Lotus Leaf Mat 4

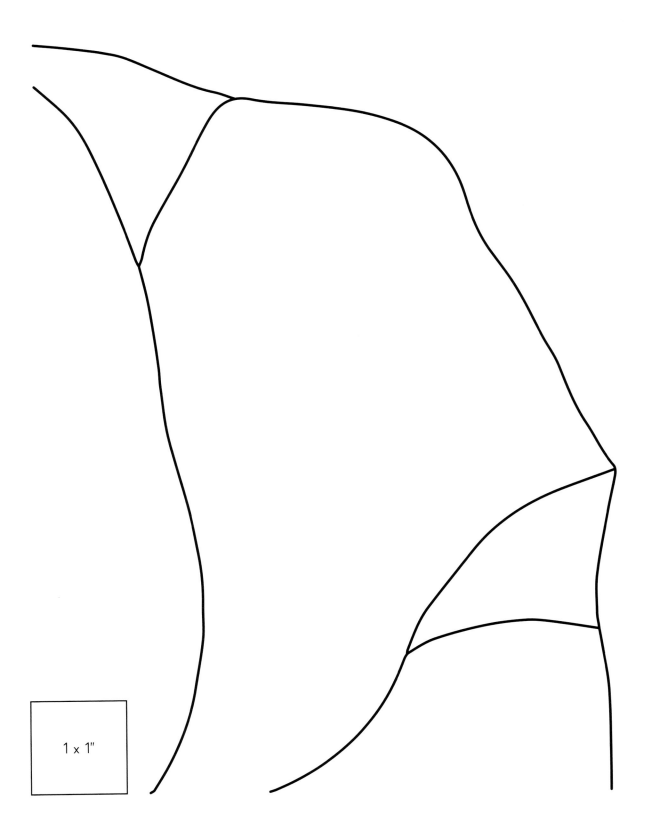

1 x 1"

Wind Chime 1
(p.124)

1 x 1"

A

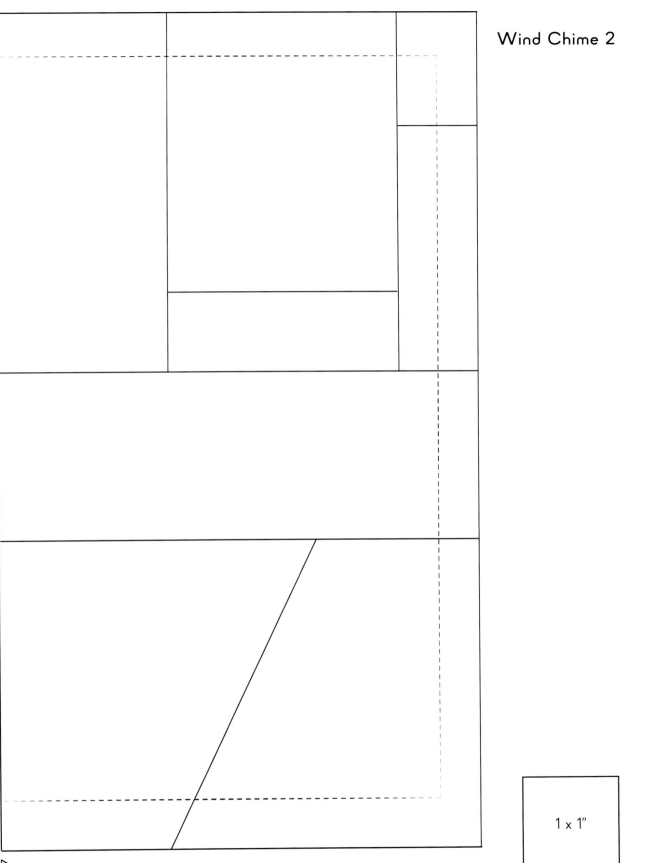

Wind Chime 2

1 x 1"

A

Covering Bojagi
(p.86)

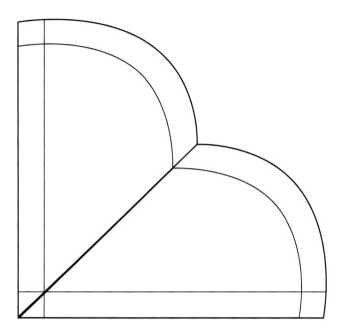

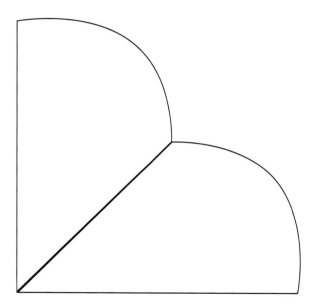

1 x 1"

Stitches

- *Homjil* 홈질 – Running stitch
- *Sichimjil* 시침질 – Basting stitch or tacking stitch
- *Gamchimjil* 감침질 – Whip stitch
- *Bageumjil* 박음질 – Back stitch
- *Ban bageumjil* 반박음질 – Half back stitch
- *Sangchim* 상침 – Top stitch
- *Gonggeureugi* 공그르기 – Blind stitch, slip stitch
- *Saebaltteugi* 새발뜨기 – Herringbone stitch
- *Satteugi* 사뜨기 – Cross stitch
- *Kkojipgi* 꼬집기 – Pin tuck stitch, pinching stitch

Solgi 솔기 – Seams

- *Hotsol* 홑솔 – A plain seam with both seam allowances lying in the same direction (hot means 'one')
- *Gareumsol* 가름솔 – Open seam
- *Tongsol* 통솔 – French seam
- *Gopsol* 곱솔, *kkekki* 깨끼 – Triple stitched seam
- *Ssamsol* 쌈솔 – Flat felled seam

Conversion Chart

Inches	mm/cm
⅛	3 mm
¼	6 mm
½	12 mm
1	2.5 cm
1¼	3.2 cm
1⅜	3.5 cm
1½	3.8 cm
2	5 cm
2½	6.4 cm
3	7.5 cm
3½	9 cm
4	10 cm
4¼	10.8 cm
4½	11.4 cm
5	12.5 cm
6	15 cm
7	18 cm
8	20 cm
8¼	21 cm
8½	22 cm
9	23 cm
10	25 cm
12	30 cm
12½	32 cm
13	33 cm
13½	34 cm
14	36 cm
15	38 cm
18	46 cm
19	48 cm
26	66 cm
30	75 cm
35	89 cm

Bibliography

Edwards, Lynne. *Cathedral Window Quilts: The Classic Folded Technique and a Wealth of Variations*. London, David & Charles, 2008.

Huh, Dong-hwa. *Bojagi's Simple Elegance*. Museum of Korean Embroidery, Seoul, 2004.

Kim, Hyun Hee. *Bojagi*. Korea Cultural Heritage Foundation, Seoul, 2000.

Kim, Jung-ho and Mi-Seok Lee. *Natural Dye and Gyubang Gongye*. Han Nam University, Daejeon, 2005.

Kim, Kumja Paik and Dong-hwa Huh. *Profusion of Color: Korean Costumes & Wrapping Cloths of the Choson Dynasty*. Asian Art Museum of San Francisco and The Museum of Korean Embroidery, Seoul, 1995.

Kim, Soo Jeong. *Embroidery in Bloom* and *Bojagi: Embracing Daily Life*. Seoul Museum of Craft Art, Seoul, 2021.

Lee, Kyung Ja, Na Young Hong and Sook Hwan Chang. *Traditional Korean Costume*. Global Oriental, Seoul, 2003.

Min, Gil-ja. *Traditional Fabrics*. Daewonsa, Seoul, 1997.

Park, Ga-young, Yeo-kyung Kim and Su-jin Song. *Chimseon: Korean Traditional Sewing*. Korea Craft and Design Foundation, Seoul, 2016.

Sim, Yeon-ok. *Weaving Hansan Semosi and Cheongyang Chunpo*. Minsokwon, Seoul, 2011.

White, Julia M., Huh Dong-hwa. *Wrappings of Happiness: A Traditional Korean Art Form*. The Honolulu Academy of Arts and The Museum of Korean Embroidery, Honolulu, 2003.

Video reference

- *Yeonbong Maedeup* (Lotus bud knot) www.youngminlee.com/video/9469
- *Dorae Maedeup* (Double crossed knot) www.youngminlee.com/video/602

Museums

South Korea

Seoul Museum of Craft Art, Seoul
craftmuseum.seoul.go.kr/eng/main

National Palace Museum, Seoul
www.gogung.go.kr/gogungEn/main/main.do

EWHA Womens University Museum, Seoul
museum.ewha.ac.kr/eng_musem/index.do

Onyang Folk Museum, Onyang
onyangmuseum.or.kr/en

Bonte Museum, Jeju
bontemuseum.com

Dankook University Seok Juseon Memorial Museum, Yongin
museum.dankook.ac.kr/en/web/museum

Sookmyeong Women's University Museum, Seoul
home.sookmyung.ac.kr/museumen/index.do

USA

Asian Art Museum, San Francisco
asianart.org

Los Angeles County Museum of Art, Los Angeles
www.lacma.org

Metropolitan Museum of Art, San Francisco
www.metmuseum.org

UK

Victoria and Albert Museum, London
www.vam.ac.uk

Places to get materials

One of the questions many people frequently ask me is, 'Where do you get your fabrics?'

Gwangjang Market in Seoul, South Korea, is the best place to shop for materials for bojagi and other Korean textile crafts and art forms. It is one of the oldest and largest traditional markets in Korea, dating back to 1905. The name Gwangjang comes from the names of two nearby bridges: Gwanggyo and Janggyo. The original market was built in between these two bridges.

When I was living and working in Seoul in the early 1990s, I often went to this market to purchase materials and to keep up with the fast-paced trends. Nowadays, when I travel to Korea every October to lead my Korea Textile Tour, I always take my people to this century-old, maze-like marketplace. I have been purchasing my materials from many stores at Gwangjang Market throughout the years, and I am happy to share a few of my favorite places with you.

Halmeoni Gapsa (Grandmother Gapsa)
Jongno 198-2 (Gwangjang market Daedong 2nd floor 503), Jongno-Gu, Seoul, South Korea
(+82) 2-2265-0201
IG: @gm.gabsa_official

WhangHae Sanghoe
Jongno 4 ga 155-3, Jongno-Gu, Seoul, South Korea
(+82) 2- 2278-8789
www.naturalkn.com   IG: @whanghae

Another big marketplace is Dongdaemun Market. This place is huge! There are four buildings connected to each other and you can find not only Korean traditional fabrics but also a variety of fabrics for garments, as well as notions, yarns and interior decorating items.
www.ddm-mall.com/eng

Acknowledgments

Writing a book in my second language was a daunting task. Even though I have so much that I want to tell you about and share with you, this project has remained a dream for a long time... until now. I am truly indebted to my family and friends for helping me overcome any and all obstacles so that I could pursue my dream project:

Sangho, who has encouraged and supported me in countless ways, since my college years until today.
Jen, you are the most reliable editor of all my writing. I am the luckiest mom to have you in my life.
Joey Colbert, a kind soul and amazing editor who took on this task at the last minute, even though she deserves her quiet retirement.
Carrie Hoge, for your beautiful photographs and friendship.

Mariah Bintliff, my dear apprentice who helped me with so many technical issues.
Meryl Macklin, for your knowledge and keen eyes.
Alex Anderson, for generously sharing your expert experience.
The Asian Art Museum and Juwon Park for image support.
My parents, who taught me perseverance and patience.
Workshop takers and newsletter readers, thank you so much for your support. I consider you all my creative community and family.

Thank you! 고맙습니다!

Photo Credits

Index